To Marija:

Expand your horizons with Indian food

Love Harry

FLAVORS FIRST

VIKAS KHANNA

AN INDIAN CHEF'S CULINARY JOURNEY

VIKAS
KHANNA

FLAVORS FIRST

LAKE ISLE PRESS, INC.
NEW YORK

Published by:
Lake Isle Press, Inc.
2095 Broadway, Suite 301
New York, NY 10023
(212) 273-0796
E-mail: lakeisle@earthlink.net

Distributed to the trade by:
National Book Network, Inc.
4501 Forbes Boulevard, Suite 200
Lanham, MD 20706
1(800) 462-6420
www.nbnbooks.com

Library of Congress Control Number: 2011927985

ISBN-13: 978-1-891105-47-0
ISBN-10: 1-891105-47-7

Book and cover design: Ellen Swandiak

Editors: Stephanie White
Jennifer Sit

First edition

Printed in the United States of America

10 9 8 7 6 5 4 3 2 1

For my Biji

CONTENTS

ACKNOWLEDGMENTS

The place I come from is grounded in tradition and I have to consciously decide which traditions to keep and which ones to let go of. The one tradition that resonates most deeply for me, which is also the purest in my mind, is the one my grandmother instilled in me as a young boy: That just as the spirit needs to be nurtured, so does food by putting flavors first. So, first and foremost, my thanks go to Biji who made me into a cook and encouraged my first efforts. Also, to my mother, for inspiring me to start the Lawrence Gardens catering company.

This book was written in collaboration with Andrew Blackmore-Dobbyn, my good friend and colleague. English is, by my reckoning, my fourth language, and I still have difficulties with the intricacies of grammar. Andrew has helped me with the language and the organization of the recipes and is a lifelong chef with whom I share cooking ideas. When I need to know how to use an unfamiliar Western ingredient, I usually talk to him first.

Flavors First is the result of my collaborations with creative cooks from around the world. These joint efforts have included Cooking for Life fundraising events that I have organized with such culinary wizards as Alain Ducasse, Jean-Georges Vongerichten, Daniel Boulud, Bobby Flay, and Drew Nieporent, among many others. I love these events most of all because we are all at our best and most charitable.

Chefs have a reputation for being temperamental and difficult to work with, but that has never been my experience. Gordon Ramsay, for example, is a warm and caring man who has helped me tremendously. Working with him on his Fox TV programs has been a life-altering experience I will never forget. Behind the scenes he cares deeply about the people around him and those people are loyal to him far beyond their professional duties. All of the chefs I have worked with are like this. When we work together on large-scale events, we all share the work, pool our knowledge, and are thus enriched. I have worked with chefs at events at the Great Pyramids of Giza, the Taj Mahal of India, and many other interesting places. During these dinners we all leave our egos outside the kitchen door. We taste each other's dishes, trade information and ideas, form new friendships, and, yes, steal each other's ideas. I am open about that, and I hope everyone knows they are welcome to my ideas as long as they are willing to share them with others. Food is meant to be shared.

I'm very proud to be a part of the wonderful team at the Rubin Museum of Art, led by special events manager Chris Phelan. My work with the museum has been one of those partnerships that has spurred all of our creativity into uncharted territory. We have catered gala dinners honoring the likes of former president Bill Clinton, Martha Stewart, the Queen of Bhutan, Sir Salman Rushdie, and Nobel Laureate Muhammed Yunus. The team also works with me on my favorite project, the Café at the Rubin Museum of Art, made possible by the generous support of Shelley and Donald Rubin.

FOREWORD

The thing that sets Vikas apart from other chefs is the force of his compassion. Many chefs make great food, and Vikas certainly does that, but he brings with him a whole culture. He never forgets that he represents Indian cuisine to many people. It is part of our strength as cooks to be so firmly rooted in our traditions. There isn't a better ambassador for Indian cuisine.

This is real cooking which is the heart and soul of what we do when we make refined cuisine. It has been my pleasure to watch Vikas create inventive new dishes that honor his past while embracing the future. This is the food that is going to shape our perception of Indian food in the world for many years to come. His passion attracts a team devoted to excellence and the true value of Indian hospitality.

We were fortunate to get Vikas to come work with us on *Hell's Kitchen* and *Kitchen Nightmares* and I hope that I have many more such opportunities in the years to come. The time we spent cooking together at my restaurant Gordon Ramsay at The London in New York taught me a great deal about the thinking of new Indian chefs. Vikas adds a dimension of humanity to the process of getting people to work harder and it has been my privilege to know him and call him a friend.

Gordon Ramsay

Introduction

My whole life is based on food. The traditions, the sharing with family and friends, the purchasing from the markets, the preparation, the festivals, weddings, and celebrations, the roadside vendors. And memories. Culture is in many ways nothing more than a vast pile of shared memories, and the cuisine of India is a reflection, even an embodiment, of all those memories. I am spiritually connected to my mother, my grandmother, ancestors now forgotten, conquerors who were themselves conquered, and to countless people and places I will never know. Recipes are handed down from one generation to the next and we add our own memories to them. These are now my memories as well. A man is a reflection of his cuisine, and his cuisine that of his culture.

In writing this book, I have tried to give an overview of some important Indian food traditions while incorporating the new foods and flavors I have learned as a result of my education and experiences in the United States. *Flavors First* is, essentially, my personal culinary journey, a variation of the journey so many immigrants make. As new immigrants come to this country, they each leave their mark on the cultural landscape, often through food. Indians are still relative newcomers compared to the Chinese and Italians who represent the two largest groups of ethnic restaurants in the country. Indian food is, however, spreading throughout the United States and I see its influence as I travel around meeting new people. In New York, there are more and better Indian restaurants that are increasingly becoming recognized for fine regional cuisine and not just the ubiquitous curry. The common link between the traditional Indian foods I grew up eating and the more cosmopolitan cuisine I prepare today are the vibrant flavors of the food. If spices are handled properly and a dish is lovingly prepared, the flavors will shine through whether you are at your own breakfast table or in the dining room of a fancy restaurant.

Flavors First, then, is the bridge between my life in India and my life in America. The recipes cover the spectrum and include some that are obviously traditional Indian dishes, some that fuse the two traditions, and some that move in a new direction. Ten years from now I am sure that Indian food will be even better known than it is already and there will be more new recipes that create Indian food from American ingredients. It's an exciting time for me and I hope to share this enthusiasm for my traditions while embracing the new ones that come my way.

To help you become more familiar with Indian cuisine, each recipe title is given in English and Hindi. In addition to recipes, I've included personal stories in this book, stories that mark important lessons I've learned about food and the ways it touches people's lives.

Spices are indispensable in Indian cuisine. They tease our senses with their enticing aromas, colors, and distinctive flavors, and they have been the catalysts for some of the greatest adventures in human history, over which fortunes were made, nations discovered, and fates met. Use this glossary to familiarize yourself with the various spices, herbs, and ingredients common to Indian cooking.

Mastering Flavors

Since spices and herbs play such a prominent role in these recipes, it's important to know what they are and how to use them. Mastering the flavors requires layering the spices and herbs in such a way that no one ingredient dominates the others.

SPICES

Spices are derived from the bark, buds, flowers, and roots of a plant. For use in Indian cuisine, I suggest always buying whole spices in small amounts, and toasting and grinding them as needed. A spice grinder or coffee grinder reserved for this purpose works well. Spices have a limited shelf life so I try not to buy more than I can use within three months. Many spices will keep longer but why take the chance? A number of specialty Indian groceries sell spices in bulk, so you can buy only what you need. If you can only find the preground spices sold at most groceries, mark the date on the label when you open the jar, so you know when its shelf life is running out.

DRY-ROASTING SPICES

The essence of many recipes lies in dry-roasting, a method that accentuates and rounds out the taste and aroma of many spices. The process releases the spices' essential oils, giving them a fuller character and a deeper, nuttier flavor.

The time it takes for dry-roasting the spices depends upon the spice being heated. Spices of similar size can be roasted together. Most nuts can also be dry-roasted.

TO DRY-ROAST: Heat a heavy-bottomed pan, such as a cast iron skillet, over medium heat until hot. Add the whole spices or nuts and roast until very fragrant and lightly browned, stirring constantly with a wooden spoon to prevent burning, roughly 2 to 5 minutes, depending on the size. Only roast as much as you need to preserve the freshness of your ingredients.

HERBS

While similar to spices, herbs come from the leaves of plants with intense flavor. Herbs are rarely the dominant flavor in a dish, but rather serve as a supporting flavor. They can be used fresh or dried and can be added whole, chopped, or even puréed. Some herbs with strong flavors, such as sage, should be added early in the cooking process while more delicate herbs, such as dill, should be added at the end to preserve their flavor. I prefer fresh herbs whenever possible. Most fresh herbs keep best on the stem. Store them covered with a plastic bag, the stem ends in a glass of water in the refrigerator. Use fresh herbs within a week of buying.

THE INDIAN KITCHEN

ASAFETIDA

Generally used in Indian vegetarian cooking, this strong smelling spice adds a deep, garlic-like flavor to recipes. Because of its strong, distinctive odor—sometimes likened to dirty socks—and flavor, asafetida should be used in small amounts. Look for ground asafetida, which mixes in rice flour and turmeric to cut the intensity, instead of the more potent lump form. Although not widely distributed, asafetida is often sold in South Asian groceries. Be sure to store in an airtight container.

BAY LEAVES

Also known as bay laurel, bay leaves are sold both fresh and dry. I use dry leaves in my recipes, which have a more distinctive, less bitter taste. Bay leaves should be removed from the dish before serving. Dry, the leaves will keep for up to a year. If they lose their olive green color and start to turn brown or yellowish, it's time to replace them. Bay leaves can be found in the spice section of most grocery stores.

BITTER GOURD

Also called bitter melon, this long fruit looks like it's covered in warts. As the fruit ripens, it grows more bitter, so it's best to eat while still green. The pith, which sweetens as the fruit ripens, can be eaten at any time.

BLACK CARDAMOM (see Cardamom) **BLACK CUMIN SEEDS** (see Cumin Seeds) **BLACK SALT** (see Salt)

CARDAMOM

These pods, the second most valuable spice after saffron, come in three different colors: mellow black, white, and pale green. The pale green is the most common and flavorful. The black seeds inside the pod hold the fragrance and are used in almost every part of Indian cuisine, from savory dishes like curries to desserts like rice pudding. Raw cardamom has a sharp, slightly bitter taste. As the spice cooks, the flavor becomes warm and sweet. The seeds are also known as "grains of heaven" for their exceptional flavor. BLACK CARDAMOM: The robust aroma of black cardamom can improve nearly any curry or meat dish. It is excellent in *biryanis* (a rice dish). Black cardamom pods can be added to soups, chowders, casseroles, and marinades for a smoky flavor. It is one of the ingredients in the recipe for garam masala, a spice blend used extensively in India.

CARAWAY SEEDS

Caraway is not used often in Indian cuisine. Its origins are believed to be in Western Asia and the Middle East. In the West it is primarily known for its role in flavoring rye bread as well as in some cheeses and pickles. In Moroccan cuisine it is used to flavor *harissa*, the hot North African chile sauce. It has a strong pungency to it and a little goes a long way.

CAROM SEEDS

These tiny seeds of the carom plant, called *ajwain* in India, resemble poppy seeds and are also known as *owa* or *omam*. They are pungent in aroma and have a sharp taste, reminiscent of thyme. I use this spice in small quantities, as it has a very strong and distinctive flavor. Normally, it is dry-roasted or fried in ghee before use.

CAYENNE PEPPER

Not a native ingredient to Indian cooking, cayenne pepper is a good substitute for Indian "chilly powder," a blend of several different dried chile peppers. I call for cayenne pepper throughout as it's more widely available. It adds a clean, clear heat to dishes without imparting much flavor of its own.

CHAAT MASALA

Chaat masala is a sweet, spicy, tangy spice mix used to flavor a variety of foods in Indian cooking, from street foods and fresh fruit to drinks.

- 2 tablespoons cumin seeds
- 1 tablespoon fennel seeds
- 1 tablespoon coriander seeds
- 1 1/2 teaspoons black peppercorns
- 1 teaspoon cayenne pepper
- 1 tablespoon carom seeds
- 1 tablespoon green cardamom pods
- 1 teaspoon red pepper flakes
- 8 to 10 whole cloves
- 1 tablespoon mango powder
- 1 dried red chile

In a heavy-bottom pan, such as a cast iron skillet, over medium-high heat, add the cumin, fennel, coriander, and peppercorns. Dry-roast until the aroma becomes highly fragrant, about 2 minutes. Remove from heat and let cool. Combine dry-roasted spices with remaining ingredients and grind to fine powder in a spice grinder. Store in a jar with a tight-fitting lid for up to 3 months.

CHILE PEPPERS, DRIED

Added to hot oil at the beginning of a dish, dried chiles add heat and flavor to the oil. Contact with the oil also intensifies the chiles—if you are sensitive to heat, I recommend removing the chiles from the dish before eating. The dried chiles most used in Indian cooking are similar to cayenne chiles or the Mexican *chile de arbol*, both of which may be used where dried red chiles are called for. These chiles are very hot and great care should be taken to avoid touching them with bare hands.

CILANTRO

In India, most street vendors include a complimentary bunch of cilantro and a handful of green chiles when you purchase groceries—these two ingredients are used extensively in our cuisine. Cilantro is used fresh and added to a dish at the last minute to preserve its fresh flavor. It keeps best refrigerated, wrapped in moist paper towels.

CINNAMON

Cinnamon, the dried inner bark of a laurel tree, plays an important role in Indian cuisine, flavoring everything from meats and curries to desserts and teas. Traditionally, whole cinnamon sticks are used in Indian cooking, but I use ground cinnamon in a few of my recipes. Ground cinnamon is available at most grocery stores but grinding your own from cinnamon sticks ensures you the freshest ground cinnamon possible.

CLOVES

Cloves are the dried, unopened buds of a tropical tree. Deep reddish-brown cloves add a strong fragrance to rice and grain recipes and are often lightly fried in hot oil, perfuming the food that is to be cooked. Cloves also serve more practical purposes: a whole clove can be used as a local anesthetic for a toothache or chewed to freshen your breath.

CORIANDER SEEDS

Coriander seeds are spherical, pale-green to beige-brown, and about the size of a peppercorn. The seeds are aromatic, with a spicy hint of lemon. Keep the seeds in small quantities in airtight containers—they lose their flavor quickly with exposure and age. Coriander seeds can also be purchased already ground (simply called ground coriander in most groceries), but as with all spices, buy whole seeds if you can, and grind as needed for best results.

COCONUT MILK

Coconut milk is not the liquid from inside a coconut. It is made by pouring boiling water over grated or shredded coconut flesh which is then squeezed to remove what is called coconut milk. It is sold in both sweetened and unsweetened varieties; only use unsweetened coconut milk in these recipes. The coconut may be subjected to subsequent rounds of steeping and straining to derive ever weaker coconut milk which accounts for the widely varying quality of this product. Use a good quality brand for best results. Coco Lopez, which is used in making tropical drinks such as piña coladas, is not coconut milk and is not suitable for any of these recipes. Take care, a sauce that contains coconut milk will eventually break if left to boil too long.

CUMIN SEEDS

Varying in color from beige to nearly black, cumin seeds have a strong, earthy taste and warm aroma; use sparingly. Often, the seeds are fried in oil at the start of a dish, infusing the ingredients to come with their flavor. Frying cumin seeds is one of the scents that most reminds me of my Biji, as she started many meals that way. If whole seeds aren't available to you, feel free to buy preground cumin seeds, simply called ground cumin. BLACK CUMIN SEEDS: The black variety of cumin seeds has a mellower flavor than regular cumin and is used to delicately flavor lentils and curries. The seeds are believed to increase heat in the body, making metabolism more efficient, and were used for medicinal purposes in ancient Egypt. It is important to note that black cumin seeds differ from nigella, or *kalonji*, another very small, very black seed.

CURRY LEAVES

Curry leaves are an integral part of Indian cooking. Mainly used as an aromatic flavoring for curries and soups, curry leaves release a fresh citrus aroma when cooked. Fresh curry leaves, which I use exclusively in these recipes, are often first fried in oil, which enhances the flavor of both the leaves and the oil. Dried curry leaves are used much like bay leaves. Fresh curry leaves can be found in the fruit section of Indian specialty food stores.

CURRY POWDER

Curry, in itself, is not a separate spice or dish. Curry, from the Tamil word *kari*, simply means sauce. The British, during their colonial rule of India, wanted to take the taste of Indian food home with them and developed curry powder. As a result curry powder in the Western world has a fairly standardized taste, but there are many varieties of curry flavors in South Asia with widely varying compositions. Most Indians don't use prepackaged curry powder, preferring to make their own blends, although it is starting to gain fans among hurried home cooks. I recommend making your own blend for the recipes in this book—this is one of the most popular variations.

1/2 cup coriander seeds

1/3 cup cumin seeds

2 tablespoons turmeric

2 tablespoons green cardamom pods

1 tablespoon cayenne pepper

1 tablespoon whole cloves

8 black peppercorns

1 tablespoon dried fenugreek leaves

Put all the ingredients in a spice grinder in batches and process at high speed until the spices are ground to a very fine powder. Store in a nonreactive (stainless steel or glass) container, covered tightly, for up to 3 months.

MADRAS CURRY POWDER

Madrassi curry powder varies from one cook to the next but the main difference in the Madrassi style is the presence of more aromatic warm spices such as cinnamon, allspice, and ginger. The recipe below has a small yield but you can easily double it if you'd like to keep some on hand.

2 tablespoons coriander seeds

1 tablespoon cumin seeds

2 teaspoon ground turmeric

1 teaspoon ground ginger

1 teaspoon cayenne pepper

1 teaspoon fenugreek seeds

1/4 teaspoon whole cloves

1/2 teaspoon ground allspice

1 teaspoon ground cinnamon

1 tablespoon black peppercorns

4 bay leaves

Put the spice mixture in a spice grinder in batches and process at high speed until the spices are ground to a very fine powder. Store in a nonreactive (stainless steel or glass) container, covered tightly, for up to 3 months.

DILL

Fresh dill has a very distinctive flavor and is often paired with fish, cucumbers, or potatoes, or added to dips, salad dressings, and cream sauces. Dill loses its flavor when heated, so always add it to cooked dishes at the last minute.

DILL SEEDS

These seeds of the dill plant are straight to slightly curved, with a ridged surface. The seeds have a much more potent flavor than the herb, similar to a combination of anise and celery.

FENUGREEK LEAVES

Called *kasoori methi*, this dried leaf lends a rich, pleasantly bitter flavor to curries. Fresh leaves are available in season and frozen leaves are also sometimes available, but I prefer the taste of the dried leaves and use them throughout. Fenugreek leaves can be found at Indian specialty food stores.

FENNEL SEEDS

For many Indians, fennel seeds are synonymous with *mukhwas*, a candy coated version of the seed with a licorice flavor that is often chewed after a meal. In cooking, the seeds are fried first to bring out the their flavor before adding to other dishes. When ground fennel is called for, it's best to buy the seeds whole and grind them yourself.

FENUGREEK SEEDS

These small seeds have a powerful, bitter taste and are used in small amounts. When frying or dry-roasting these seeds, take care not to overcook—the seeds will become excessively bitter and inedible.

GARAM MASALA

Garam masala is the most important spice blend in North Indian cuisine. Adding a little pinch of garam masala at the end of cooking or right before serving adds more flavor to the dish.

- 3 tablespoons green cardamom pods
- 2 black cardamom pods
- 1 tablespoon black peppercorns
- 1 tablespoon whole cloves
- 1 teaspoon ground ginger
- 1 teaspoon coriander seeds
- 2 tablespoons ground cinnamon
- 1/4 teaspoon mace flakes
- 2 bay leaves

Preheat the oven to 300°F. Put all the ingredients on a large baking sheet and roast until the spices become very fragrant, about 5 minutes.

Put the spice mixture in a spice grinder in batches and process at high speed until spices are ground to a fine powder. Store in a nonreactive (stainless steel or glass) container, covered tightly, for up to 3 months.

GHEE

Also known as clarified butter, ghee is butter that has been melted down to separate the milk solids and water from the butterfat. After melting and sitting over low heat, the water evaporates, and a few milk solids float to the surface (and are skimmed off), while the remainder of the heavier milk solids sink to the bottom. The butterfat, clear and yellow, is poured off the top and preserved, leaving the whey to be discarded. Ghee can be purchased in jars from Indian groceries but is not difficult to make. Allow for about 25% loss to the skimming process when calculating how much you need to make. Ghee keeps well in the refrigerator, up to six months, but it will absorb refrigerator odors if not properly sealed. Ghee gives a clean butter flavor and burns at a much higher temperature than whole butter. It also can be kept for a time at room temperature which makes it preferable in a warm climate where refrigeration is a luxury.

GINGER

A paste of puréed ginger and garlic starts many Indian dishes. Ginger is used frequently for its rich, pungent aroma and peppery bite. Fresh ginger is best when the roots are firm and the knobs snap when broken. Dried, ground ginger should have an intense gingery aroma.

GRAM (CHICKPEA) FLOUR

Used in many Indian recipes, especially *dosas*, gram flour is made from ground dried chickpeas. It can be found in Indian groceries, health food stores, and some gourmet shops.

HIMALAYAN SALT (see Salt)

LONG BLACK PEPPER (see Peppercorns)

MADRAS CURRY POWDER (see Curry Powder)

GREEN CHILE PEPPERS

Chiles are one of the most important ingredients for pungency and heat in Indian cuisine. In most regions, they are served raw on the side as an accompaniment to the meal. To reduce the heat of the peppers, remove the seeds and ribs and only use the green outer flesh. Thai chiles, the very small, very hot, pointed chiles we generally use in Indian cuisine are not typically available in grocery stores, but you may be able to find them in East Asian groceries. I often suggest serrano peppers as a substitute, as they are readily available, though they're not as hot. Be careful when handling any hot pepper. Wash your hands immediately after touching as the oils in the pepper can burn your skin. If you're working with a particularly hot pepper, wear gloves to be safe.

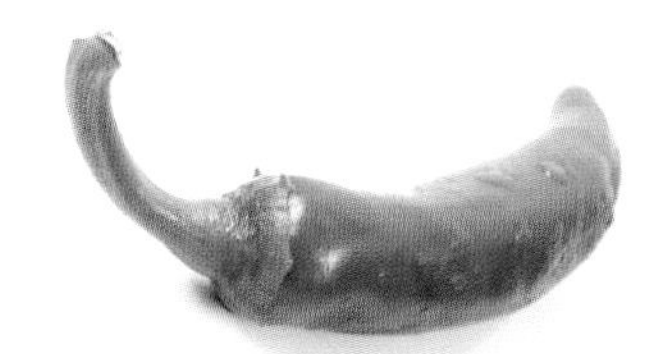

MACE

Mace, the dried, amber-colored covering of the nutmeg seed, tastes similar to nutmeg, but with a more intense flavor. Mace is available as flakes or blades and ground—buy the flakes or blades for the best flavor.

MANGO POWDER

The dried pulp of green (unripe) mangoes is ground to make mango or *amchoor* powder. It is beige in color, slightly fibrous in appearance, and sweet-and-sour in taste. It is used particularly to add tartness to a dish such as a salad or *chaat*. It is available in South Asian groceries.

MINT

Mint, a popular herb known for its sweet taste and cool finish, is used in a variety of dishes and drinks. While fresh mint is preferred, I do occasionally use dried mint for making breads. Fresh and dried mint can be found in most groceries.

MUSTARD SEEDS

Many varieties of mustard seeds are available, but black seeds are the most commonly used in Indian cooking. Black seeds are used to make mustard oil, a pungent oil with a strong taste. For the most part, I use whole mustard seeds in these dishes, frying them briefly in oil to start a dish, but ground mustard seeds are also sometimes used. Note that prepared Western mustards are not an effective substitute for mustard seeds in any of these recipes.

NIGELLA SEEDS

Nigella, known as *kalonji* in South Asia, is an essential ingredient in the Bengali five-spice mix, *panch phoran*. The small black seeds look like black sesame seeds and are also considered important in ayurvedic practice. The use of nigella as a medicine is believed to go all the way back to ancient Egypt—nigella seeds were found in the tomb of Tutankhamen. Confusingly, this spice is sometimes mistakenly referred to as black onion seed, black sesame, and black cumin.

NUTMEG

The rich brown seed of the fruit of a tropical evergreen, nutmeg has a warm, sweetly spicy flavor used to season both savory and sweet dishes. It is available in whole and ground forms. For best results, I always prefer buying it whole and then freshly grating or grinding it according to the recipe. A microplane grater works well for this task.

PANEER

Paneer is a type of fresh cheese popular in Indian cuisine. The curds are separated from hot milk by adding lemon juice or another food acid. The curds are then drained in cheesecloth, resulting a solid cheese. Paneer can be purchased from Indian groceries.

PAPRIKA

A spice made by grinding dried mild chiles, paprika is used in many different cuisines. The Indian variety is called *Kashmiri mirch*; mild Hungarian paprika also works well in these recipes.

PANCH PHORAN

Also known as five-spice mix, *panch phoran* is a traditional Bengali spice mix and quintessential flavoring in Eastern Indian cuisines. It lends a lovely aroma to dishes and is used whole, without grinding. Typically, the spice mix is fried in oil at the beginning of a dish.

1 teaspoon fennel seeds

1 teaspoon nigella seeds

1 teaspoon fenugreek seeds

1 teaspoon black mustard seeds

1 teaspoon cumin seeds

Combine all ingredients. Store in an airtight container for up to three months.

PEPPERCORNS

Although peppercorns have made their way into cuisines all over the world, black peppercorns are native to India. These small berries of a pepper plant are picked at various stages of ripeness and dried to varying degrees which creates different varieties and flavors, from very hot and a little plain tasting to sweet, complex, and aromatic. I prefer black peppercorns in most of my dishes for their deep, mellow flavor. For chutneys, I often use pickled green peppercorns, which have a lighter, more ethereal taste. LONG BLACK PEPPER: Long black pepper, known as *pippali* in India, is a close relative of the black pepper plant and has a similar, though generally more floral essence. Because of this floral character and much higher price it is used less than black peppercorns. It has a similar appearance to black peppercorns with longer peppers. It should be freshly ground when used. TELLICHERRY PEPPERCORN: The favored black peppercorn of chefs all over the world is the Tellicherry, which comes from Kerala in India. They have a heady, sweet aroma and a deep, rich flavor.

POMEGRANATE SEEDS, DRIED

These sundried, kernel-like seeds of the wild Indian pomegranate have a sour, tangy flavor and impart a dark brown color to curries when cooked in hot oil. When a recipe calls for ground dried pomegranate seeds, buy the dried seeds whole and grind them as needed. Fresh pomegranate seeds can not be substituted for the dried ones.

ROSE BUDS, DRIED

Rose buds have been used for centuries in Indian and Middle Eastern cuisines for the aromatic, floral flavor they add to food. They have a very soft texture and swell up in curries. They are sold whole and are available in Middle Eastern and South Asian groceries.

ROSE SPREAD (GULKAND)

Rose spread is a preserve of rose petals in syrup and is used in desserts and as a palate cleanser. The Indian holistic tradition of Ayurveda uses the rose for its soothing and cooling effect on the mind and body. Rose spread is found in South Asian groceries.

ROSE WATER

Rose water, essentially rose petals cooked in water, is sometimes distilled to give it a purer, more concentrated floral flavor. It imparts an intoxicating scent of roses to rice dishes, desserts, and drinks. When using rose water for the first time, use a light hand until you are familiar with the floral flavor. I recommend buying rose water rather than making your own; store-bought roses are often sprayed with pesticides. Rose water is available at Indian groceries.

SAFFRON

Saffron is the world's most expensive spice and with good reason: one pound of saffron requires almost seventy-five thousand handpicked blossoms. From those blossoms, the stigmas are removed and dried. Saffron has a distinctively warm, rich, powerful, and intense flavor. It can be purchased in strands or ground. I recommend strands for the sake of quality. My grandmother kept a private supply of saffron that she used to mark special occasions. On my birthday, she would mix a little saffron with water and mark my forehead with it. Eventually that saffron always ended up in my mouth.

SALT

Salt is the world's oldest known food additive and comes in many varieties. For seasoning most dishes any salt will do. When cooking in the restaurant kitchen, I like the feel of kosher salt in my fingers but for table service we use Himalayan salt. BLACK SALT: Despite its name, black salt is more salmon-pink in color, sometimes even appearing gray. Popular in Indian food, black salt adds an earthy, sulfurous flavor to street snacks, savory drinks, and fruits. First time users beware: this strong flavor won't appeal to all Western palates. Look for black salt in South Asian groceries and spice shops. HIMALAYAN SALT: Himalayan salt has been a part of my pantry ever since I lived in Nepal. The salt adds a wonderful aroma and earthy taste to food and can be found at many specialty stores.

STAR ANISE

These star-shaped pods have a pronounced licorice flavor, stronger than fennel or anise seed. I add whole star anise to dishes like curries to add dimension to the flavor. Star anise can also be used to flavor sweet dishes.

TAMARIND

The sticky, sour pulp from the tamarind bean pod is used in chutneys and assorted preserves. Available both as a pressed slab (which still contains the seeds from the tamarind pod) and bottled concentrate, I recommend the bottled concentrate, sold as tamarind paste in Indian groceries.

TELLICHERRY PEPPERCORN (see Peppercorns)

TURMERIC

Turmeric is what gives curry powder its characteristic color. Related to ginger, this root is used in ground form. It has a deep, astringent flavor, indispensible to Indian cuisine. While traveling in Tibet, I was surprised to learn that turmeric is primarily used as a medicine there and must be bought in a natural remedy pharmacy.

CONDIMENTS

The abundant use of condiments in Indian cooking truly makes it unique. Pickled condiments are generally served on the side to balance the palate and lighten the flavors of the dish. Chutneys are versatile, so feel free to experiment with different fruits and vegetables to suit the season or your tastes.

...

The beauty of these recipes is that you can prepare them in advance and store them—they become even more flavorful over time. I like to make them in bulk and give them away as gifts.

BLUEBERRY CHUTNEY with ORANGE ZEST

APPLE and CINNAMON MURABBA

SWEET EGGPLANT CHUTNEY

TOMATO and TELLICHERRY PEPPERCORN CHUTNEY

MIXED BERRY SALSA with LIME DRESSING

MANGO and PASSION FRUIT SAUCE

MANGO-LEMON CHUTNEY with PISTACHIOS

ORANGE-GINGER CHUTNEY

BEET and POPPY SEED CHUTNEY

GINGER-CILANTRO PESTO with TOASTED WALNUTS

OKRA RAITA with MUSTARD SEEDS

PEAR and TAMARIND CHUTNEY

CILANTRO CHUTNEY

Blueberry aur Santra chhilke Chutney

BLUEBERRY CHUTNEY WITH ORANGE ZEST

4 cups fresh or frozen blueberries

1 (16-ounce) can whole berry cranberry sauce

1/4 cup sugar

3 tablespoons balsamic vinegar

1 1/2 teaspoons grated orange zest

1/2 teaspoon freshly ground black pepper

Fresh blueberries are incorporated into this unique take on a traditional chutney. The orange zest enlivens and adds depth to the flavor. I make this sauce a day or two ahead and store it in the refrigerator. It tastes great with flatbreads. | makes about 2 1/2 cups

1. Combine all ingredients in a saucepan over medium heat and cook uncovered until the mixture comes to a boil. Reduce heat to low and simmer, stirring constantly, until thickened, about 20 minutes. Remove from heat.

2. Let cool briefly, then purée half of the chutney in a blender and return it to the saucepan to cool to room temperature.

3. Pour into clean jars, cover, and refrigerate for up to 3 weeks.

Seb ka Murraba

APPLE & CINNAMON MURABBA

Murabba, a condiment made from fruits or vegetables, originated in Gujarat, in northwest India. Sugar works as the preserving agent in these addictive dishes. Traditionally *murabba* is eaten as a roadside snack or during festivals, but I like to serve it with grilled meats or even desserts. | makes about 2 cups

- 3 red apples, peeled, cored and cut into 1-inch cubes
- 2/3 cup sugar
- 6 tablespoons water
- 4 green cardamom pods
- One 2-inch-long cinnamon stick
- 5 whole cloves
- Juice of 1 lemon

1. Gently prick the apple cubes all over with a fork.

2. In a heavy-bottom pan, bring the sugar, water, cardamom, cinnamon, and cloves to a boil. Add the apples, reduce the heat, and cook until the apple cubes become translucent and plump, 10 to 12 minutes. Remove from heat and stir in the lemon juice.

3. Let cool before storing in an airtight container. The *murabba* will keep for up to 6 months in the refrigerator. Serve warm or cold.

Food Rituals

I was blessed as a young person to know what I wanted to be when I grew up. I knew it with a sense of certainty that has never left me. Seeing the everyday food rituals performed by my grandmother, whom we respectfully called Biji, was a moment of truth in my life, something so profound that it left a permanent impression on my mind.

It was an everyday, but sacred ritual: Biji purchased, cooked, and served food that nurtured not only her family but also friends, neighbors, and strangers. Each day when we came home from school, the meals were ready on a hot plate or skillet we call a *tawa*. The cast iron *tawa* was locally made and kept hot with charcoal. That rusted plate became for me a symbol of generations of love and care. Biji prepared traditional foods for us and since we had no refrigeration, shopping and cooking had to be done each day. As we served ourselves from the hot *tawa*, she would make fresh *roti* breads, one at a time. By the time you finished your first *roti*, the second was on your plate, effortlessly and perfectly timed—a skill that I took for granted until I learned to do it myself.

After Biji fed us lunch, she would nap for an hour and then be back in the kitchen making afternoon tea for everyone. I watched her, sipping her tea, getting ready for the evening meal: cutting vegetables, rinsing rice, shelling the fresh peas, or sorting the lentils. Her wrinkled hands, having performed these same rituals for so many years, moved effortlessly.

Once she began cooking dinner, I had my Biji all to myself. That was when I learned what it meant to be a cook. Though Biji was vegetarian, on Sundays she cooked meat for us. Since she couldn't taste the meat, she called on me to check the *masala*, the balance of salt and pungency. It was always a moment of pride and a special treat for me to be the one to approve the seasoning, all the while learning how to taste the balance of meat and spices we used. Biji nurtured the cook within me and knew my calling even before I did. As smells of dinner drew my family near, the ritual was complete for another day. The following morning it started all over again.

Meethi Baingan Chutney

SWEET EGGPLANT CHUTNEY

Baby eggplants are the perfect choice for this easy chutney recipe. The tender-skinned baby eggplant is sweeter and contains fewer seeds than larger varieties, and its subtle flavor is enhanced by spices such as cumin, nigella, and turmeric as well as a red wine vinegar and garlic sauce. Brown sugar adds richness. The result just melts in your mouth. Serve with roasted or curried poultry. | makes 4 cups

- 1/2 cup packed light brown sugar
- 1/3 cup red wine vinegar
- 6 cloves garlic
- One 2-inch-long piece fresh ginger, peeled and coarsely chopped
- 2 tablespoons vegetable or canola oil
- 2 teaspoons cumin seeds
- 1 tablespoon nigella seeds
- 2 dried red chile peppers
- 1 teaspoon ground turmeric
- 1 medium tomato, diced
- 1 pound baby eggplant (about 10), cut lengthwise into quarters but not through the stem end
- 1 1/2 cups water
- 2 tablespoons honey
- 1 teaspoon salt
- Juice of 1 lemon

1. In a blender or a food processor, blend the brown sugar, vinegar, garlic, and ginger until smooth.

2. In a medium, heavy-bottom pan with a lid, heat the oil over medium heat. Add the cumin seeds, nigella seeds, and chiles and cook until fragrant, about 1 minute. Stir in the sugar-vinegar mixture and the remaining ingredients. Bring it to a boil, reduce heat to low, cover, and simmer until the eggplant is tender and cooked through, about 20 minutes. Let cool, uncovered, to room temperature and adjust salt to taste. Store, refrigerated, in an airtight container for up to 2 weeks.

- 2 teaspoons black mustard seeds
- 2 teaspoons minced fresh curry leaves
- 3 whole dried red chile peppers
- 2 large cloves garlic, minced
- 1 medium red onion, finely chopped
- 1 tablespoon ground coriander
- 1 teaspoon ground cumin
- 1 tablespoon Tellicherry peppercorns, ground
- 3 tablespoons vegetable oil
- 1 teaspoon paprika
- 1/2 teaspoon salt
- 1 (28-ounce) can plum tomatoes, drained and chopped
- 2 tablespoons tomato paste
- 2 tablespoons red wine vinegar

Tamatar ke Saath Tellicherry Kali Mirch

TOMATO & TELLICHERRY PEPPERCORN CHUTNEY

Tellicherry peppercorns are well worth seeking out—their elegant aroma and unique pungency add sophisticated flavor. The peppercorns come from the tiny Tellicherry region of the Malabar coast of India. This recipe makes a savory tomato chutney that is very addictive. Serve it alongside meat or even use it as a marinade. | makes 1 1/2 cups

Heat the oil in a small saucepan over medium heat and add the mustard seeds, curry leaves, and chile peppers. Add the garlic and onion, sauté briefly to soften the onion, then add the coriander, cumin, ground peppercorns, paprika, and salt and continue cooking another 2 minutes. Add the chopped tomato, tomato paste, and vinegar and bring to a boil. Reduce the heat to low and cook, stirring occasionally, until the mixture is reduced and thickened, 10 to 15 minutes. Serve hot or cold. Store, refrigerated, in an airtight container for up to 2 weeks.

Taaza Berry Chaat

MIXED BERRY SALSA WITH LIME DRESSING

- Juice of 1 lime
- 2 tablespoons honey
- 1 cup fresh blueberries
- 1 cup fresh strawberries, coarsely chopped
- 1 cup fresh raspberries
- 1 cup fresh blackberries
- 1 small jalapeño pepper, seeded and minced
- 1/4 cup chopped fresh mint leaves
- 1 teaspoon *chaat masala* (page 20)

Chaat masala adds key notes of sweet and sour to this salsa along with a touch of honey and a variety of berries. The jalapeño adds a nice piquant flavor. Try to make the salsa and dressing at least an hour before serving to give the flavors time to marry. *Chaat masala* is generally used as a seasoning on roadside snacks in India, but can also be found alongside appetizers or salads. | makes about 4 cups

In a medium bowl, whisk together the lime juice and honey until thoroughly combined. Add the remaining ingredients and gently toss to coat. Store in an airtight container in the refrigerator for up to 2 days.

Aam aur Krishna Fal Chutney

MANGO & PASSION FRUIT SAUCE

- 4 fresh passion fruits
- 2 tablespoons unsalted butter
- 2 whole star anise
- 1/2 cup sugar
- 1 cup canned mango purée (found at Indian groceries)

This sweet-tart sauce pairs well with cheesecake or vanilla ice cream. | makes 2 cups

1. Cut the passion fruit in half and scrape out the pulp and seeds; discard skin.

2. Melt the butter in a medium saucepan on medium heat and fry the star anise until fragrant, about 1 minute. Add the sugar, passion fruit pulp and seeds, and mango purée and cook, stirring, until the flavors are combined and sugar is dissolved, 4 to 5 minutes.

3. Cool to room temperature. The sauce can be kept for about a week refrigerated or 4 months when frozen.

Pista -Aam -Nimboo Chutney

MANGO-LEMON CHUTNEY WITH PISTACHIOS

- 1/4 cup shelled whole pistachios
- 6 fresh mangoes, ripe but still firm
- 1 cup cider vinegar
- 1 cup sugar
- Juice of 2 lemons
- 1 teaspoon salt

Lemon juice tempers the sweetness of the mango and gives it a light, crisp flavor while the vinegar tenderizes the fruit and gives it an extra tang. This chutney has a somewhat mild taste and goes well with fish dishes. | makes 2 cups

1. Preheat the oven to 325°F. Spread the pistachios out in a single layer on a baking sheet and toast until lightly browned and fragrant, 5 to 6 minutes.

2. Peel the mangoes and cut the flesh into 1-inch cubes. Place all the ingredients in a medium saucepan and bring to a boil. Reduce the heat to low and simmer gently, stirring occasionally, until the mixture is thick, about 30 minutes. Adjust salt to taste.

3. Let cool to room temperature and store in the refrigerator in an airtight container for up to 1 week.

Santray aur Adrak ki Chutney

ORANGE-GINGER CHUTNEY

2 large oranges

1 tablespoon vegetable oil

One 2-inch-long piece fresh ginger, peeled and minced

1 medium yellow onion, finely chopped

1/4 teaspoon salt

1 teaspoon red chile flakes

1/2 cup apple cider vinegar

1/2 cup packed light brown sugar

The citrus tang of orange with the spiciness of ginger makes for a warm and refreshing combination that complements grilled meats and vegetables. | **makes about 2 1/2 cups**

1. Use a microplane (or other fine grater) to remove 1 tablespoon zest from the oranges and set zest aside. Cut away the remaining peel and pith from the oranges. Cut the individual segments over a bowl, retaining all the juice. Remove and discard the seeds.

2. Heat the oil in a saucepan over medium heat; add the ginger, onion, salt, and chile flakes and cook, stirring, for 2 minutes. Add the orange segments, reserved juice and zest, the vinegar, and brown sugar and bring to a boil. Lower the heat and simmer, stirring occasionally, until thickened, 20 to 25 minutes.

3. Remove from heat. Let cool to room temperature, and refrigerate in an airtight container for up to 2 weeks.

Chukandar ke Saath Khuskhus

BEET & POPPY SEED CHUTNEY

This recipe was in a book of notes from my grandmother and has an amazing taste. The texture can be adjusted to your liking—I prefer it chunky, speckled with poppy seeds. Sweetened with honey, this lemony chutney goes well with grilled fish, but can also be tossed in a salad to add texture and color. | makes 2 cups

- 1 tablespoon olive oil
- 2 tablespoons poppy seeds
- 1 pound beets, peeled and cut into 1-inch cubes (about 2 cups)
- 3 1/3 cups water
- 3 tablespoons honey
- 1/2 teaspoon salt
- Juice of 1 lemon

1. In a medium, heavy-bottom pan, heat the oil over medium heat. Add the poppy seeds and cook, stirring, for 1 minute. Add the beets and cook until well coated with seeds. Increase the heat to high and add the water, honey, and salt and bring to a boil. Reduce the heat to medium and simmer until the beets are tender and cooked through, about 20 minutes. Add additional water if needed to keep a syrupy consistency. Remove from heat.

2. Add the lemon juice and stir well. Let cool, uncovered, to room temperature and store in the refrigerator in an airtight glass container (the beets will stain any other type of container) for up to 2 weeks.

Adrak-Dhaniya aur Bhune Akhrot

GINGER-CILANTRO PESTO WITH TOASTED WALNUTS

- 1 cup walnuts pieces, toasted and cooled
- 4 cups (about 1/4 pound) tightly packed fresh cilantro leaves
- One 2-inch-long piece fresh ginger, peeled and coarsely chopped
- 2 cloves garlic, coarsely chopped
- Salt and freshly ground black pepper
- 2/3 cup extra-virgin olive oil

This variation on classic pesto is made with cilantro, ginger, and walnuts. Toasting the walnuts brings out their rich aroma and taste while ginger and garlic give the pesto an extra zip. I like to have a jar of this pesto in my refrigerator to use as a sandwich spread or dip for appetizers. | makes about 2 cups

In a food processor, combine the walnuts, cilantro, ginger, and garlic. Season generously with salt and pepper. Pulse quickly a few times until the nuts are finely chopped. With the machine running, pour oil in a steady stream through the feed tube; blend until smooth. Adjust the salt and pepper to taste. Store in a clean jar and refrigerate for 3 to 4 days.

Bhindi ka Raita

OKRA RAITA WITH MUSTARD SEEDS

- 1/2 pound fresh okra
- 2 tablespoons vegetable oil
- 1 tablespoon black mustard seeds
- 1 teaspoon cumin seeds
- 1 dried red chile, split in half lengthwise
- 1/2 teaspoon ground asafetida
- 4 fresh curry leaves
- 1/2 teaspoon salt
- 1 1/2 cups plain, lowfat yogurt, whisked smooth

This dish is popular in Kerala, in the south of India. The okra and nutty-tasting mustard seeds make a great combination. *Raita*, essentially a chutney with yogurt, is the perfect condiment to serve with breads or curries. | serves 4

1. Clean the okra with a wet kitchen towel and pat dry. Cut into 1-inch pieces and set aside.

2. Heat the oil in a small pan with a lid over medium heat and fry the mustard seeds, cumin seeds, chile, asafetida, and curry leaves until the mustard seeds begin to crackle, about 2 minutes. Reduce the heat to low, add the okra and salt and stir until the okra is well coated with oil. Cover and cook over low heat until the okra is tender and cooked through, about 15 minutes. Remove from heat and let cool to room temperature.

3. Add the cooked okra to the yogurt and season with salt to taste. Store in an airtight container in the refrigerator for about a week.

Nashpati-Imli Chutney

PEAR & TAMARIND CHUTNEY

The tangy, sour taste of tamarind marries well with the sweetness of the pear. I recommend this as an accompaniment to lamb, but it also goes well with chicken. My sister, Radhika, likes this with eggs for breakfast. | **makes about 2 1/2 cups**

- 2 tablespoons vegetable oil
- 1 tablespoon black mustard seeds
- 4 firm-ripe pears, cored and cut into 1-inch cubes
- 1/2 teaspoon ground cinnamon
- 1/4 cup tamarind paste
- 1/2 cup sugar
- 1/2 teaspoon salt
- 1 cup water

1. Heat the oil over medium heat in a medium, heavy-bottom pan with a lid. Add the mustard seeds and stir for 1 minute. Add the pears and cook until well coated with the seeds. Add the cinnamon, tamarind paste, sugar, salt, and water, and bring to a boil. Reduce the heat, and simmer, covered, until the pears are cooked through and the liquid is syrupy, about 20 minutes. Add additional water if needed.

2. Remove from heat and let cool to room temperature, uncovered. Adjust salt to taste. Store, refrigerated, in an airtight container for up to 2 weeks.

- 1 large bunch cilantro, washed and roughly chopped (about 2 ounces)
- 6 scallions, coarsely chopped
- 2 hot green chile peppers (such as serrano or Thai), roughly chopped
- 1 teaspoon sugar
- 2 tablespoons peeled, chopped fresh ginger
- 1 teaspoon ground cumin
- 1 teaspoon salt
- 1/4 cup fresh lemon juice
- 1/4 cup extra virgin olive oil

Hare Dhaniya ki Chutney

CILANTRO CHUTNEY

Cilantro chutney is always a crowd favorite—it goes well with a variety of dishes and makes a great dip for appetizers. Try it with Chicken with Tellicherry Pepper and Caramelized Onions (page 186). | makes about 2 cups

Place all ingredients except the olive oil in a blender. Blend at medium speed, slowly drizzling in the olive oil, until smooth. Store, refrigerated, in an airtight container for up to 3 days.

STARTERS

Inspired by regional street foods, these smaller plates can be enjoyed on their own any time of the day or as a complement to a meal. I encourage you to be playful with how you assemble your starters; they give you a chance to wow your guests and give a good impression of the meal to come.

• • •

Most of the recipes in this chapter can be prepared in advance and then easily warmed up or fried before serving.

FRIED DUMPLINGS STUFFED WITH PEAS AND RAISINS

PLANTAIN AND SPINACH FRITTERS

WONTON CRISPS WITH TAMARIND CHUTNEY AND PINEAPPLE

CRISPY PAN-FRIED SHRIMP

SAMOSAS WITH SPICED GROUND CHICKEN AND PEAS

AMRITSAR-STYLE BATTER-FRIED FISH

MINT-FLAVORED GRILLED CHICKEN

POTATO CAKES WITH CUMIN

MUNG BEAN AND SPINACH TURNOVERS

TURMERIC- AND GINGER-SCENTED PANEER SHASHLIK

JALAPEÑOS STUFFED WITH CASHEWS AND COCONUT

DEEP-FRIED HARDBOILED EGGS

PAN-SEARED LEMON CURRY SCALLOPS

LAMB KEBABS WITH PEANUT SAUCE

Gujrati Kachori

FRIED DUMPLINGS STUFFED WITH PEAS & RAISINS

These dumplings, known as *kachoris*, are a popular North Indian snack. When I was young, on my way home from school I would stop and eat *kachoris* almost every day. The crispy-flaky crust and the filling of peas combined with spices and sweet raisins were a gourmet delight for me; even today they are one of my favorite snacks. | makes 20 *kachoris*

FOR THE DOUGH

- 1 1/4 cups all-purpose flour, plus more for dusting
- 2 tablespoons vegetable oil, plus more for bowl, work surface, and hands
- 2 tablespoons plain, lowfat yogurt, whisked smooth
- 1 teaspoon caraway seeds
- 1/2 teaspoon salt
- 1/3 cup water

FOR THE FILLING

- 1 pound russet potatoes (about 3 medium potatoes)
- 1/2 cup fresh or frozen peas, thawed, coarsely mashed
- 3 tablespoons golden raisins
- 2 tablespoons chopped fresh cilantro
- 1 teaspoon cayenne pepper
- 1 teaspoon cumin seeds, dry-roasted (see page 17) and finely ground
- 1 teaspoon garam masala (page 25)
- 1/2 teaspoon salt
- Vegetable oil, for deep-frying
- Tamarind Chutney (page 57), for serving

1. To start the dough, put the flour in a large bowl and mix in the vegetable oil, yogurt, caraway seeds, salt, and water. Knead well until soft, smooth, and elastic, about 5 minutes. Form the dough into a ball and transfer it to a clean, lightly oiled bowl. Cover the bowl with plastic wrap or a clean kitchen towel and let rest for 30 minutes.

2. Meanwhile, make the filling: Boil the potatoes in their skins until tender, about 30 minutes. Let the potatoes cool until they can be handled: peel the potatoes and mash them in medium bowl.

3. Add the peas, raisins, cilantro, cayenne pepper, cumin, garam masala, and salt and mix well.

4. Turn the dough out of the bowl onto a lightly oiled work surface and divide it into 20 equal pieces. Roll the pieces into balls. On a lightly floured surface, flatten the balls into 2-inch disks with a rolling pin.

5. Place 1 tablespoon of the filling in the middle of each disk. Grease your hands lightly (this will keep the dough from sticking to your hands) and wrap the dough around the filling so it forms a smooth ball.

6. Line a sheet pan with paper towels. Heat a heavy-bottom pot filled with about 3 inches of oil over medium heat to 300°F. If you don't have a thermometer, test the oil by dropping in a small piece of dough. The oil is ready if the dough bubbles immediately upon contact. Gently slide 6 to 8 dumplings into the oil, occasionally pressing them down with a slotted spoon until they puff slightly. Flip the dumplings over to fry the other side until golden brown and crisp, 4 to 5 minutes. Drain on lined baking sheet. Repeat until all dumplings are fried.

7. Serve hot with chutney on the side for dipping.

Kele-Palak ke Pakore

PLANTAIN & SPINACH FRITTERS

As a child, my head barely reached the top of the kitchen counter, so my grandmother would sit me down on the white marble countertop, and from there I would observe her for hours, asking questions constantly and stealing bites of the savories she prepared. When she poured the fresh oil into her gleaming stainless steel wok and started frying plantain fritters, to my young eyes they seemed like flowers floating in a pool of gold. Try these fritters once and you will be hooked, too. | serves 4

- 1 cup gram (chickpea) flour
- 1/4 teaspoon baking powder
- 1/2 teaspoon salt
- 1 medium egg
- 1 teaspoon cayenne pepper
- 1/2 teaspoon ground asafetida
- 1/2 teaspoon ground turmeric
- 1/2 cup water
- 2 yellow plantains, peeled and coarsely grated (see Note)
- 10 ounces frozen chopped spinach, defrosted and wrung dry in a kitchen towel (see Note)
- Vegetable oil, for deep-frying
- Naan (page 102), for serving (optional)

1. In a medium bowl, sift the flour with the baking powder and salt. Add the egg, cayenne pepper, asafetida, turmeric, and water and whisk vigorously, blending until smooth. Fold the grated plantains and spinach into the fritter batter and gently combine.

2. Line a sheet pan with paper towels. Heat a deep-fryer or a large saucepan filled with at least 2 inches of oil to about 350°F. If you don't have a thermometer, test the oil by dropping in a small piece of batter. The oil is ready if the batter bubbles immediately upon contact with the oil and floats. Drop the fritter batter into the hot oil by the spoonful (about 2 tablespoons each), 8 to 10 fritters at a time, and cook for 3 to 5 minutes, turning once to evenly brown. Remove the fritters from the oil, and drain on the lined sheet pan.

3. Serve warm with naan, if desired.

notes: Be sure your plantains are yellow and haven't started to turn black. As plantains ripen, they go from green (starchy) to yellow (sweet, like bananas) to black (mushy). Yellow plantains have the right taste and texture for this recipe. • Fresh spinach can also be used. Sauté 1 pound of fresh spinach, well washed, in 1 tablespoon olive oil until wilted. Let the spinach cool, then squeeze dry and chop finely.

Delhi Papri Chaat

WONTON CRISPS WITH TAMARIND CHUTNEY & PINEAPPLE

- 1 large potato
- 20 square wonton wrappers, thoroughly defrosted if frozen
- Vegetable oil, for deep-frying
- 1 cup plain, lowfat yogurt, whisked smooth
- 1/2 teaspoon salt
- 1 tablespoon cumin seeds, dry-roasted (see page 17) and ground
- 1 teaspoon sugar
- 1 teaspoon cayenne pepper
- 1 medium onion, finely chopped
- 1 (15-ounce) can chickpeas, drained and rinsed
- 1/2 cup Tamarind Chutney (recipe follows)
- 1/2 cup diced fresh or canned pineapple
- 2 tablespoons chopped fresh cilantro, for garnish

I use wonton skins to simplify the preparation of this dish; using canned chickpeas is another great shortcut. Yogurt adds a silky texture to the crisps and combines well with aromatic ground, roasted cumin seeds. Sweet-and-sour tamarind chutney rounds out the dish. | serves 6

1. Boil the potato until tender, about 30 minutes. Let cool: peel and cut into 1/2-inch cubes.

2. Line a sheet pan with paper towels. Cut the wonton wrappers into 1-inch-long strips about 1/2-inch wide. Pour 3 inches of oil into a heavy pot and heat to 350°F over medium heat. If you don't have a thermometer, test the temperature by dropping a piece of wonton wrapper into the oil. It should bubble immediately. Fry the wonton strips until crisp and golden brown, 1 1/2 to 2 minutes. Remove with a slotted spoon and drain on lined sheet pan.

3. Whisk together the yogurt, salt, cumin, sugar, and cayenne pepper in a small bowl; set aside. In a medium bowl, gently mix together the diced potato, onion, and chickpeas.

4. On a serving plate, spread half of the crispy wonton strips for the first layer. Place the potato mixture over it. Arrange the remaining strips over the potato mixture. Layer the yogurt mixture, chutney, and pineapple chunks over the crispy wonton strips. Serve immediately, garnished with cilantro.

1 tablespoon vegetable oil
1 teaspoon cumin seeds
1 teaspoon ground ginger
1/2 teaspoon cayenne pepper
1/2 teaspoon fennel seeds
2 cups water
1 cup sugar
1/4 cup tamarind paste
1/2 teaspoon salt

TAMARIND CHUTNEY

makes about 2 cups

Heat the oil in a saucepan over medium heat. Add the cumin seeds, ginger, cayenne pepper, and fennel seeds, stirring until fragrant, about 2 minutes. Add the water, sugar, and tamarind paste. Bring to a boil, and then simmer over low heat until the mixture turns a deep brown and is thick enough to coat the back of a spoon, 20 to 30 minutes. Let it cool to room temperature before serving and season with salt, adjusting to taste.

A Guilty Pleasure

Only very rarely did my family go out to restaurants. It was an extravagance to us and with a cook like my Biji at home we were not going to get any food better than hers. The exceptions were the sweets shops which made things Biji did not usually make at home. Mathura Sweets Shop and Bansal Sweets were gourmet heavens to me. I was a scraggly boy of ten when the guys at Bansal Sweets mistook me for a beggar staring at the treats and gave me a bag of leftovers. Although I clearly knew they had made a mistake, I thought, what the hell, let me enjoy it just this one time. I ate enough that day to make my belly ache, but not without a delicious feeling of guilt. Biji would have been horrified if she had known. I felt too guilty to ever do it again. Instead, I learned to taste food just by the smell, passing by roadside kiosks and sweet shops and inhaling deeply. I thought that it was the best way to taste as it was free.

Karara Jhinga

CRISPY PAN-FRIED SHRIMP

- One inch-piece fresh ginger, peeled and finely chopped
- 2 cloves garlic, chopped
- 1 teaspoon ground cumin
- 2 tablespoons tamarind paste
- 1 teaspoon cayenne pepper
- 1/2 teaspoon ground turmeric
- 2 tablespoons all-purpose flour
- 1/4 teaspoon salt
- 6 tablespoons vegetable oil
- 1 pound small shrimp, shelled and deveined
- Basmati rice (page 78), optional

Shrimp, fish, and other seafood are plentiful in South India, where this dish originates. In this recipe, garlic and tamarind paste add an exotic blend of tart and spicy without overpowering the delicate shrimp. Serve the shrimp on their own as a starter or with basmati rice for a nice meal. | serves 6

1. Mix the ginger and garlic with cumin in a large bowl. Add the tamarind paste, cayenne pepper, turmeric, flour, and salt. Blend 2 tablespoons oil into the mixture. Pat the shrimp dry with a paper towel and add to spice mixture; toss well to coat evenly. Cover and refrigerate 1 to 3 hours (not longer).

2. Line a sheet pan with paper towels. Heat the remaining 4 tablespoons oil in a large saucepan over medium heat. Gently add the marinated shrimp and cook for 1 minute on high heat. Turn the shrimp over and cook for another minute. Reduce the heat and cook for 2 to 3 minutes, until opaque, turning the shrimp occasionally for uniform cooking. Remove and drain shrimp on the lined sheet pan.

3. Serve hot with basmati rice, if desired.

Murg Samosa

SAMOSAS WITH SPICED GROUND CHICKEN & PEAS

Most old cultures in the world have some form of filled, wrapped, fried, or baked pastry. In India, we have samosas, the most common appetizers in Indian restaurants. I often add leftover vegetables to the filling. You will be surprised how easy it is to make these crisp golden brown samosas yourself. | makes 10 samosas

FOR THE PASTRY:

- 2 cups all-purpose flour, plus more for dusting
- 1/4 teaspoon salt
- 1/4 cup ghee
- About 2/3 cup cold water

FOR THE FILLING:

- 2 tablespoons ghee
- 1 medium onion, minced
- One 1-inch-long piece fresh ginger, peeled and minced
- 1 tablespoon minced garlic
- 1 fresh green chile pepper (such as serrano), seeded and finely minced
- 1 teaspoon ground coriander
- 1 teaspoon garam masala (page 25)
- 1 teaspoon cumin seeds
- 1/4 teaspoon ground turmeric
- 1 1/3 pounds ground chicken
- 1/2 cup fresh or frozen peas, thawed
- 1 teaspoon salt
- 1/4 cup water
- 1/4 cup finely chopped fresh cilantro
- Juice of 1 lemon
- Vegetable oil, for deep-frying
- Tomato and Tellicherry Peppercorn Chutney (page 40), for serving

1. To make the pastry, combine the flour and salt and then rub the ghee into the flour until well combined and the mixture resembles coarse crumbs. Add the water, 1 tablespoon at a time, until the pastry comes together to form a ball. The dough should be somewhat soft and elastic. Knead the dough lightly and then form into a ball; wrap in plastic wrap and transfer to the refrigerator for 1 hour or up to 2 days.

2. To make the filling, heat the ghee in a medium skillet with a lid over medium-high heat and add the onion. Cook, stirring continuously, until the onion is lightly caramelized, about 5 minutes. Add the ginger, garlic, green chile, coriander, garam masala, cumin seeds, and turmeric, and cook until the spices are fragrant, about 2 minutes. Add the chicken, peas, salt, and water; reduce the heat to medium, cover, and cook, stirring occasionally, until the meat is very tender and the water has been absorbed, about 20 minutes. Stir in the cilantro and lemon juice and set aside to cool completely.

3. Divide the samosa dough into 10 portions and roll each into a ball. On a lightly floured surface, use a rolling pin to roll each ball into a 5-inch circle. (Use a small bowl or the rim of a saucer and a sharp paring knife to trim the edges of the dough to form neat circles.) Cut each circle in half. Lightly moisten half of the straight edge of each half-circle then bring the corners together, one on top of the other, and seal the edges together to form a cone. Carefully spoon about 2 heaping tablespoons of the filling into the dough cone and push downward to compress the filling. Moisten the top edges of the dough with a bit of water and press together to seal. Repeat with the remaining portions of dough and filling.

4. Line a sheet pan with paper towels. Heat a deep-fryer or a large saucepan filled with at least 3 inches of oil to about 325°F. If you don't have a thermometer, test the temperature by dropping in a small piece of dough. It should bubble immediately if the oil is ready. Fry the samosas, stirring and flipping them to promote even cooking, until the pastry is crispy and golden brown, 4 to 5 minutes. Remove with a slotted spoon and transfer to lined pan to drain.

5. Serve hot with chutney.

Amritsari Machhi

AMRITSAR-STYLE BATTER-FRIED FISH

Growing up in Amritsar, a city in northwestern India known for its hospitality and food, I was always amazed by the roadside restaurants, known as *dhabas*, famous nationwide for their fresh and delicious food. Chiman Lal is one such popular roadside restaurant in Amritsar, from which this batter-fried fish recipe originates. Other restaurants serve this fish, but Chiman Lal's recipe is the best. It took me many years to get one of the chefs to reveal the secret recipe. It is simple to make and a great appetizer. You can serve it with any chutney of your choice. | serves 4 to 6

- 1 1/2 pounds fresh cod, monkfish, or salmon
- 1 teaspoon fresh lemon juice
- 1 teaspoon minced garlic
- 1/2 teaspoon salt
- 1 tablespoon ground fennel
- 1/2 teaspoon carom seeds
- 1 teaspoon cayenne pepper
- 1/2 cup all-purpose flour
- 1/2 cup water
- Vegetable oil, for frying
- 2 cups plain bread crumbs
- 1 teaspoon mango powder

1. Wash the fish and pat dry. Cut into 1-inch pieces. Rub with lemon juice, garlic, and salt. Cover and set aside in the refrigerator for at least 2 hours or overnight.

2. In a medium, nonreactive (stainless steel or glass) mixing bowl, combine the fennel, carom seeds, cayenne pepper, and flour. Pour in water gradually and whisk until smooth. The consistency should be like thick pancake batter. Set aside for 20 minutes.

3. Line a sheet pan with paper towels. Heat a deep-fryer or a large saucepan filled with at least 3 inches of oil to about 350°F. Test the oil by adding a few drops of batter. If the oil is hot enough, the batter will sizzle on contact and begin to brown within 5 seconds. Place the bread crumbs in a bowl or shallow dish. Dip a few pieces of fish into the batter and thoroughly coat them. Using your fingers, coat the fish with bread crumbs. Gently set the coated fish into the hot oil and fry for 5 minutes, turning once, until lightly golden brown. Remove the fish from the oil and drain on the lined sheet pan.

4. Serve hot, sprinkled with mango powder.

Pudinewala Murg

MINT-FLAVORED GRILLED CHICKEN

- 1 medium red onion, peeled and coarsely chopped
- 2 tablespoons finely chopped garlic
- 1 cup tightly packed fresh mint leaves
- 1/2 teaspoon freshly ground black pepper
- 1 teaspoon garam masala (page 25)
- 1 tablespoon fresh lemon juice
- 1 teaspoon salt
- 1 pound boneless, skinless chicken breast, cut into 1-inch strips, lengthwise
- 20 medium bamboo skewers
- Orange-Ginger Chutney (page 44)

Though fresh mint is often used in Indian cooking in chutneys and summer drinks, in this recipe, I have used mint in a marinade for the chicken giving it a similar fresh pop. Shrimp or vegetables can be substituted for the chicken. | serves 4

1. Mince the onion in a food processor or blender. Add the garlic, mint leaves, pepper, garam masala, lemon juice, and salt. Mince again, and transfer to a large, nonreactive (stainless steel or glass) mixing bowl, reserving 1/4 cup of marinade for basting. Add the chicken and toss well to coat evenly. Cover and refrigerate for 1 to 3 hours.

2. Soak the skewers in water for at least 15 minutes before you start to thread them. Preheat a gas grill for 15 minutes on high or prepare a charcoal fire. Thread the chicken onto the skewers through its deepest part. Grill over medium to medium-low heat until cooked through and still tender, 10 to 12 minutes, basting with the reserved marinade and turning occasionally to ensure even cooking. Try to turn the skewers as little as possible when cooking so the chicken doesn't stick to the grill.

3. Serve hot with the chutney.

The End of Ice Cream

My family used to make the most wonderful hand-churned mango ice cream at home with Biji. It always took such a long time to make, so we took turns sitting on the ground in the courtyard, cranking the churn, inevitably fighting over who got to go next. Biji would keep us waiting, sitting in a circle, making it take longer than it really needed to. I didn't understand then, but Biji showed us that the anticipation was a big part of the joy. My sister would crack jokes as each person's arm got tired and we'd laugh and roll around like little fools. When the ice cream was finally frozen, it was the highlight of the day.

When one day we bought an electric ice cream machine, Biji shook her head, left the room, and no amount of coaxing would get her to look at it. When we finally got her to even talk about it, she said that it was "the end of ice cream." She was right. We only used the machine twice, but all the fun was gone—no more joking around, no more fighting over having a turn with the crank. The machine was soon forgotten and we never made ice cream again. I learned that as technology makes cooking easier in some ways, it can also take away the unexpected joys that come from old-fashioned work.

Aloo Sooji ki Tikki

POTATO CAKES WITH CUMIN

To celebrate the rich heritage of the Taj Mahal, a ten-day carnival called Taj Mahotsav is held annually near the monument. One of my favorite dishes at the festival is the local delicacy: potato cakes with cumin. At the festival, the cakes are made on a cast-iron Indian *tawa* (similar to a griddle) and topped with red onions and chutneys. These potato cakes can be made ahead and rewarmed or served at room temperature. | serves 6

- 1 pound russet or red boiling potatoes (about 3 medium potatoes)
- About 1 teaspoon salt, plus more for boiling potatoes
- 1/4 cup all-purpose flour
- 1 cup semolina flour
- 2 fresh green chile peppers (such as serrano), seeded and finely chopped
- 1 medium Spanish onion, finely chopped
- 1 teaspoon ground cumin
- 1 teaspoon cayenne pepper
- 1/2 cup chopped fresh cilantro
- Vegetable oil, for frying
- Ginger-Cilantro Pesto with Toasted Walnuts (page 46), for serving

1. Boil the potatoes in salted water until tender, about 30 minutes. Remove from water and let sit until cool enough to handle. Peel potatoes and cut them in half. Pass the potatoes through a potato ricer or grate them on the large holes of a box grater. Place in a bowl.

2. Add the flour, semolina, green chiles, onion, cumin, cayenne pepper, cilantro, and salt. Knead until smooth. Divide the mixture into 12 equal pieces. Take a portion and flatten it on your palm, shaping into a 1/2-inch thick cake.

3. Line a sheet pan with paper towels. Heat a deep-fryer or a large saucepan filled with at least 2 inches of oil to about 350°F. Test the oil by dropping in a small piece of potato cake. If the oil is ready, the cake should float and begin to brown within 5 seconds. Gently drop the cakes, in batches of 4 to 6, into the hot oil, cooking for 5 minutes and turning them occasionally to brown evenly. Remove from the oil and drain on lined sheet pan

4. Serve hot topped with pesto.

Daal aur Pakora Samosa

MUNG BEAN & SPINACH TURNOVERS

- 2 tablespoons vegetable oil, plus more for baking sheet
- 1 teaspoon cumin seeds
- 1 1/2 tablespoons peeled, minced fresh ginger
- 1 fresh green chile pepper, (such as serrano), minced
- 1 tablespoon ground coriander
- 1 1/4 cups dried mung beans, washed, soaked overnight, and drained
- 1/4 teaspoon ground turmeric
- 1/2 teaspoon salt
- 1 cup water
- 1 cup chopped fresh spinach
- 6 phyllo pastry sheets
- 2 tablespoons melted butter
- 1 medium egg, beaten

This is one of my favorite stuffings for phyllo dough. If the phyllo is frozen, it should be completely defrosted before being handled. Once removed from the package, the phyllo needs to be covered with a damp towel to prevent it from drying out. The mung beans need to soak overnight, so plan ahead. For make-ahead appetizers, these can be baked, frozen, and reheated at 375°F for five to eight minutes. | serves 6

1. Preheat the oven to 350°F. Heat the oil in a large, nonstick saucepan with a lid over medium heat and add the cumin seeds, ginger, green chile, and coriander. Stir for about 30 seconds. Mix in the mung beans, turmeric, and salt and cook, stirring, about 2 minutes. Add the water, lower the heat to medium-low, cover the pan, and cook until all the water has been absorbed and the beans are soft, 10 to 15 minutes. Add the spinach and stir until wilted, about 1 minute. Remove from heat and let cool.

2. Grease a baking sheet with oil. Brush each phyllo sheet with melted butter, stacking one on top of the other. With a sharp knife, cut lengthwise into 4 strips, each about 3 inches wide. Stack again and cut each strip into 6 squares. Cover with a clean damp kitchen towel.

3. Place a phyllo square on the work surface and spoon a generous tablespoon of the filling in the center. Brush the egg all around the edges of the square and fold into a triangle, pressing edges together to seal the filling. Repeat until all the dough is gone. Place the turnovers on the baking sheet and brush with the remaining egg. Bake until crisp and golden, about 20 minutes. Transfer to cooling racks. Serve warm or at room temperature.

Adraki Paneer

TURMERIC- & GINGER-SCENTED PANEER SHASHLIK

- 3 cups plain, lowfat yogurt
- 1 teaspoon ground turmeric
- One 1-inch-long piece fresh ginger, peeled and minced
- 4 cloves garlic, minced
- 2 tablespoons fresh lemon juice
- 5 tablespoons fresh lemon thyme leaves, chopped
- 1 teaspoon salt
- 10 ounces paneer, diced
- 2 green bell peppers, diced
- 1 medium onion, diced
- 2 firm tomatoes, diced
- 2 tablespoons vegetable oil
- 8 metal skewers

Shashliks, foods cooked on skewers, make a delicious snack. In this case, paneer cheese is marinated with vegetables and then broiled on skewers. I usually choose organic, locally grown produce from the farmers' market when buying the seasonal vegetables for this recipe. The marinade can be made in advance and kept for three to four weeks refrigerated. | serves 4

1. Line a colander with multiple layers of cheesecloth and set it over a large bowl. Add the yogurt, and let it drain for about 6 hours in the refrigerator. The result will be about 1 1/2 cups of thick yogurt.

2. Mix the yogurt, turmeric, ginger, garlic, lemon juice, lemon thyme, and salt in a large bowl. Add the paneer and vegetables to the marinade, cover, and refrigerate for 3 to 4 hours.

3. Preheat the broiler. Thread the paneer, peppers, onions, and tomatoes evenly onto metal skewers. Brush with oil. Broil for 3 to 4 minutes on each side, or until the paneer and vegetables are cooked and slightly charred around the edges. Serve hot.

Kaju aur nariyalwali Bhari Mirchi

JALAPEÑOS STUFFED WITH CASHEWS & COCONUT

The taste of sweetened coconut flakes with spicy peppers makes this a perfect appetizer for spice lovers. | makes 24 peppers

- Vegetable-oil cooking spray
- 1 pound russet potatoes (about 3 medium potatoes)
- 1/3 cup raw cashews, coarsely chopped
- 1/3 cup sweetened coconut flakes
- 1 teaspoon ground cumin
- 1 1/2 teaspoons salt
- 12 jalapeño peppers (see Note)
- 1/2 cup gram (chickpea) flour
- 1/2 cup all-purpose flour
- 1 teaspoon carom seeds
- 1/4 cup water
- Vegetable oil, for frying

1. Preheat the oven to 350°F. Spray a baking sheet with oil and arrange the potatoes on top. Bake until a bit overcooked, about 45 minutes. Let sit until cool enough to handle, then peel and cut in half. Pass the potatoes through a potato ricer or grate them on the large holes of a box grater. Place potatoes in a medium mixing bowl.

2. Combine the potatoes, cashews, coconut, cumin, and 1 teaspoon salt. Cut a short slit into each jalapeño pepper. Remove as many seeds as possible with a small spoon. Stuff the jalapeños with the potato mixture.

3. In a small bowl combine both flours, the carom seeds, and the remaining 1/2 teaspoon salt and mix well. Slowly add the water, about 1/4 cup, to the flour mixture, whisking constantly, until the batter has a slightly thickened and very smooth consistency.

4. Line a baking sheet with paper towels. Heat a deep-fryer or a large saucepan filled with at least 2 inches of oil to about 350°F. Test the oil by putting a few drops of batter in the oil. The batter should begin to bubble and brown within 1 minute. Dip the jalapeños in the batter and carefully drop them into the hot oil, frying in batches of 6 to 8 at a time; cook for 5 to 7 minutes, turning to brown evenly. Remove from the oil and drain on lined baking sheet. Serve hot.

note: Wear latex gloves when removing the seeds or be careful not to touch the seeds with your bare fingers—the seeds can burn. Wash your hands well immediately after handling.

- 18 ounces lean ground lamb
- 2 teaspoons ground cumin
- 2 tablespoons ground coriander
- 2 tablespoons finely chopped fresh cilantro
- 1 tablespoon plain, lowfat yogurt
- 1 tablespoon finely chopped garlic
- 1 tablespoon garam masala (page 25)
- 1 teaspoon curry powder (page 23)
- 1 medium red onion, finely chopped
- 1 egg, lightly beaten
- 1/2 teaspoon salt
- 1/2 teaspoon freshly ground black pepper
- 10 hardboiled eggs, peeled
- Vegetable oil, for frying, plus more for rolling the meat

Nargisi Kofta

DEEP-FRIED HARDBOILED EGGS

This dish, known as *nargisi kofta*, is quite like Scotch eggs. Refrigerating the meat after seasoning it helps to create a firm shape around the eggs. This is a great party appetizer and can be served at room temperature. | makes 10

1. Combine all the ingredients except for the hard-boiled eggs and oil in a large, nonreactive (stainless steel or glass) mixing bowl. Cover and refrigerate for 30 minutes.

2. Divide the seasoned meat into 10 equal portions. Using oiled hands, evenly shape the meat around the hardboiled eggs.

3. Line a sheet pan with paper towel. Fill a wok with 3 inches oil and heat oil to 375°F. Test the oil by dropping a small piece of meat into the wok. If the meat sizzles on contact, the oil is hot enough. Fry the meat-coated eggs until golden brown, gently turning them for even cooking. Remove with a slotted spoon and drain on lined sheet pan. Serve hot.

Nimboo Masala Scallops

PAN-SEARED LEMON CURRY SCALLOPS

- 1 tablespoon butter
- 2 shallots, peeled and finely diced
- 1 tablespoon Thai green curry paste
- 1 teaspoon finely chopped lemongrass, tough outer leaves discarded
- 1 cup unsweetened coconut milk
- Zest and juice of 1/2 lemon
- 2 tablespoons vegetable oil
- 18 large sea scallops, cleaned and patted dry
- 2 tablespoons fresh cilantro leaves, for garnish
- 1 lime, cut into wedges, for garnish

This simple lemon curry sauce comes together in minutes. I use larger sea scallops for this recipe and have found that three scallops make a nice appetizer portion. | serves 6 people as an appetizer

1. Combine the butter, shallots, curry paste, and lemongrass in a small saucepan over medium-low heat. Cook until the edges of the shallots turn golden brown, about 4 minutes. Stir in the coconut milk and simmer for 2 minutes before stirring in the lemon juice and zest.

2. Preheat a heavy sauté pan over medium heat and add the vegetable oil, heating until hot but not smoking. Pan-sear the scallops for 2 to 3 minutes, on each side, until nicely browned. Remove the scallops to serving dishes. Spoon a little of the creamy sauce over each scallop, garnish with the chopped cilantro and lime wedges, and pass the rest of the sauce separately.

Mungfali ki chutney ke sath

LAMB KEBABS WITH PEANUT SAUCE

A warm Asian flavor combined with a peanut sauce has made these kebabs popular with my guests. Yogurt tenderizes the meat and ginger adds a very aromatic note to this dish. Both components can be made well in advance and frozen for later use. | serves 4

FOR THE KEBABS

- 5 cloves garlic, crushed
- One 2-inch-long piece fresh ginger, peeled and finely chopped
- 2 fresh green chile peppers (such as serrano), seeded and finely chopped
- 1 medium red onion, chopped
- 3 tablespoons plain, lowfat yogurt
- 1/4 cup packed fresh cilantro leaves
- 1 pound lean ground lamb
- 1 teaspoon salt
- 1 tablespoon Thai red curry paste
- 1 tablespoon green Tabasco sauce, or other green chile sauce
- Lemon wedges, for garnish
- 4 metal skewers

FOR THE PEANUT SAUCE

- 1 (13 1/2-ounce) can unsweetened coconut milk
- 1 tablespoon light brown sugar
- 1 teaspoon ground cumin
- 1 tablespoon Thai red curry paste
- 1/2 cup chunky peanut butter

1. To make the kebabs, combine the garlic, ginger, green chiles, onion, yogurt, and cilantro in a food processor and blend to form a smooth paste. In a large bowl, mix the paste with the ground lamb, salt, curry paste, and Tabasco sauce. Mix well. Shape the meat into 16 oval patties, about 2 inches long, then cover and chill for 1 hour.

2. Meanwhile, make the sauce: In a saucepan, combine the coconut milk, brown sugar, cumin, and curry paste over medium heat. Bring to a boil and reduce heat to low. Add the peanut butter, whisking thoroughly until smooth. Continue to cook until flavors are well blended, about 3 minutes. Remove from heat.

3. Preheat the broiler. Thread 4 patties onto each skewer. Broil until slightly brown on top, 7 to 10 minutes. Turn over and cook the other side, about 2 minutes. Serve hot with peanut sauce on the side for dipping.

RICE

Rice is almost sacred in Indian cuisine; it is used in many religious ceremonies and is prepared daily in virtually every Indian home. On my travels throughout the East I have been influenced by varieties from other regions, Bhutanese red rice and Chinese forbidden rice, for example, and I have included these grains in the following recipes.

• • •

Many of these grains can be found in ethnic grocery stores. Be sure to check expiration dates whenever you buy prepackaged rice—it can, and will, go bad. These rice dishes pair perfectly with the main dishes and condiments in this cookbook or can be meals on their own.

BASMATI RICE

BASMATI RICE WITH RAISINS AND PISTACHIOS

SAFFRON, CRANBERRY, AND CARDAMOM PULAO

LENTILS AND RICE WITH VEGETABLES

LEMON, PEANUTS, AND CURRY-LEAF PULAO

MINT PULAO WITH FRESH POMEGRANATE SEEDS

DUM LAMB BIRYANI WITH SAFFRON

BASMATI RICE WITH DRY-ROASTED SPICES

HIMALAYAN RED RICE VEGETABLE PULAO

FORBIDDEN RICE AND PEAS PULAO

SPINACH AND PANEER CHEESE PULAO

BROWN BASMATI WITH CARAMELIZED ONIONS AND BROCCOLI

CHAI-INFUSED EMPEROR'S GREEN RICE

Basmati chawal

BASMATI RICE

India is the world's largest producer of aromatic, long-grain basmati rice. It is famously grown in the foothills of the Himalayas. American-grown basmati rice is widely available in grocery stores and is an adequate substitute for Indian basmati. | makes 4 servings

1 cup basmati rice

1 tablespoon butter

1 1/2 cups water

1/2 teaspoon salt

1. Wash the rice in a sieve under cool running water until the water runs clear, about two to three minutes. Set rice aside.

2. Heat a small, heavy-bottom saucepan over medium heat. Melt the butter in the pan and add the rice, stirring until the rice is well coated, about 2 minutes. Add the water and bring to a boil. Reduce the heat to low and cover tightly. Let the rice simmer without touching it for about 17 minutes. Remove the rice from the heat and let sit for five minutes more, then fluff the rice with a fork and serve.

Saugi-Pista Pulao

BASMATI RICE WITH RAISINS & PISTACHIOS

- 2 cups water
- 1 1/2 cups basmati rice, rinsed with cold water and drained
- 1 teaspoon salt
- 1 teaspoon dry-roasted cumin seeds (see page 17)
- 3 tablespoons vegetable oil
- 1 cup shelled, raw pistachios
- 1 cup raisins
- 1/4 cup raw almond slivers
- 1 clove garlic, minced
- 2 fresh green chile peppers (such as serrano), finely chopped
- 1 tablespoon honey
- 1/2 cup sweetened coconut flakes

Raisins, pistachios, almonds, and a dash of honey make for a colorful and fancy dish for special occasions. | serves 4

1. In a medium saucepan with a lid over high heat, bring the water to a boil; add the rice, salt, and cumin seeds. Return to a boil, then reduce the heat to low, cover, and simmer until the water is absorbed and the rice is tender, 10 to 15 minutes. Transfer to a large bowl and keep warm.

2. In a large saucepan over medium-high heat, combine the oil, pistachios, raisins, and almonds and cook until the raisins swell and become fragrant, 4 to 5 minutes. Transfer to the rice bowl.

3. Using the same pan over medium-high heat, add the garlic, green chiles, and honey. Stir continuously for 2 minutes. Remove from the heat, add the rice and the pistachio mixture, and mix well.

4. Serve hot, garnished with coconut flakes.

Zaffran-Elaichi Pulao

SAFFRON, CRANBERRY & CARDAMOM PULAO

- 1 1/4 cups basmati rice
- 2 tablespoons vegetable oil or ghee
- Two 1-inch-long cinnamon sticks
- 4 green cardamom pods
- 1/2 teaspoon whole black peppercorns
- 1 large red onion, thinly sliced
- 1/2 tablespoon peeled, minced fresh ginger
- 1/2 tablespoon minced garlic
- 1 teaspoon saffron threads
- 1/2 cup dried cranberries, plus a few more for garnish
- 2 1/3 cups water
- 1/4 cup finely chopped fresh cilantro, for garnish

Saffron-scented basmati rice is combined with cranberry, cinnamon, and cardamom in this traditional, slightly sweet dish. I use dried cranberries as an alternative to raisins to add flavor, texture, and rich color. Add to that the earthy aroma of cardamom and the slightly bittersweet taste of cinnamon, and this fabulous *pulao* is a great accompaniment to any meal. | serves 6

1. Rinse the rice with cold water to remove the excess starch; drain. Soak the rice in cold water for 30 to 45 minutes. Drain and set aside.

2. In a large pot with a lid, heat the oil or the ghee over medium-high heat and cook the cinnamon, cardamom pods, and black peppercorns until fragrant, about 1 minute. Add the onion and cook, stirring, until golden, about 5 minutes. Mix in the ginger, garlic, and saffron and stir for about 2 minutes. Then add the rice, cranberries, and water, and bring to a boil. Reduce the heat and simmer, covered, until all the water has been absorbed and the rice is done, 12 to 15 minutes.

3. Serve hot, garnished with fresh cilantro and dried cranberries.

Subzi wali Khichdi

LENTILS & RICE WITH VEGETABLES

Considered an Indian comfort food, this is the dish my mother always made for me when I was sick as a child. The texture is similar to risotto. In this version, I have added broccoli, carrots, and peas to the basmati rice and lentils. When preparing this dish in the U.S., I use French green lentils. | serves 6

- 1 cup basmati rice
- 2 tablespoons ghee or vegetable oil
- 1 teaspoon cumin seeds
- 1/4 teaspoon ground asafetida
- 1 cup green lentils
- 1 teaspoon ground turmeric
- 1 teaspoon salt
- 4 cups water
- 1/2 cup coarsely chopped broccoli
- 1 cup cauliflower florets
- 1/2 cup fresh or frozen peas, thawed
- 1/2 cup chopped carrots
- Juice of 1 lime

1. Rinse the rice with cold water to remove the excess starch; drain. Soak the rice in cold water for 30 to 45 minutes. Drain and set aside.

2. Heat the ghee or oil over medium heat in a medium pot with a lid. Add the cumin seeds and asafetida and cook, stirring, until fragrant, about 1 minute. Add the rice, lentils, turmeric, and salt and stir continuously until well mixed. Add the water, bring to a boil, and then reduce the heat to low. Add the broccoli, cauliflower, peas, and carrots and stir well. Cover and cook until the mixture has a thick, risotto-like consistency, 15 to 20 minutes. Using a whisk, mix the rice and stir in the lime juice. Serve hot.

Potato Curry or Curry Potato

Every day of my childhood passed by with new culinary experiences and adventures, but as time went on, I had to learn some very hard lessons about food as well. In 1984, not long after my first cooking disaster, a state of emergency was declared in the state of Punjab due to Operation Blue Star, an Indian military operation. Within Punjab, we lived in the city of Amritsar, the very center of the conflict. The army sealed us off from the rest of the world for many weeks, cutting water, electricity, and food supplies. We were left with nothing but a large bag of potatoes to feed the entire family.

People around us were soon starving. Every day we had to eat the same dish of potatoes, and finally one evening, I pushed my plate away. Out of youthful ignorance, I refused to eat another plate of potato curry. My Biji looked at me and smiled. She said, "Oh no, Viku, this is not 'potato curry.' This is 'curry potato.'" I ate.

Many years have passed and times have changed, but remembering Biji's sorrowful smile still breaks my heart. In that moment, she redefined food for me. She knew that with food, when we give ourselves over to the making of it, we are giving our spiritual energy too. Even in that terrible time, she still wanted to give me the best she had.

I became more acutely aware of how many people in India and the world lived in a state of near-starvation every day of their lives. By these standards, my family was quite well off—though we had few luxuries, we never faced true hunger outside of that military operation.

Food is a blessing and I try never to forget this. Biji taught me that I could make the most exotic and expensive meal in the world, but it means little if I don't find it in my heart to share what I have with those in need.

Nimboo, Moongfali, Curry-Patta Pulao

LEMON, PEANUTS & CURRY-LEAF PULAO

- 1 cup basmati rice, rinsed under cold water several times and drained
- 4 cups water
- 1 teaspoon ground turmeric
- 1/2 teaspoon salt
- 2 tablespoons vegetable oil
- 2 teaspoons black mustard seeds
- 2 fresh green chile peppers (such as serrano), seeded and minced
- 5 tablespoons unsalted, raw, skinless peanuts
- 2 dried hot red chile peppers (such as *chile de arbol*), crushed
- 1/4 teaspoon ground asafetida
- 6 fresh curry leaves
- Juice of 1 lemon

Lemon rice, or *yelumiccha pazha sadham*, as it's called in the Tamil language, is a very popular rice dish in the South Indian region of Tamil Nadu. Served at auspicious functions, festivals, and as an offering at temples, this dish has a special place in my heart. This recipe has a light lemon flavor, a seasoning of fragrant curry leaves infused in oil, and a peanut crunch. The number of chiles called for makes this a fairly spicy dish for average tastes, so feel free to use fewer. | serves 4

1. In a medium saucepan over high heat, boil the rice, uncovered, in the water with the turmeric and salt for about 10 minutes. Drain, and cover to keep warm.

2. Heat the oil in a heavy-bottom skillet over medium heat. Add the mustard seeds and stir until crackling, about 2 minutes. Add the green chiles, peanuts, red chiles, asafetida, and curry leaves and cook, stirring continuously, until very fragrant, 2 to 3 minutes. Stir in the rice and evenly mix all the ingredients.

3. Remove from heat, stir in the lemon juice, and adjust the salt to taste. Serve hot.

Pudina- Anar Pulao

MINT PULAO WITH FRESH POMEGRANATE SEEDS

- 2 tablespoons vegetable oil
- 1 small red onion, thinly sliced
- 1 small Idaho potato, peeled and cut into 1/2-inch slices
- 1 1/2 tablespoons peeled, minced fresh ginger
- 2 tablespoons coarsely chopped fresh mint leaves
- 1 fresh green chile pepper (such as serrano), minced
- 1 1/4 cups basmati rice, rinsed under cold water several times and drained
- 2 1/4 cups water
- 1/4 teaspoon salt
- 2 teaspoons cumin seeds, dry-roasted (see page 17) and coarsely crushed
- 1 cup fresh pomegranate seeds

The minty flavor and the crunch of fresh pomegranate seeds make this a palate-pleasing dish. To remove pomegranate seeds from the shell, I cut the fruit in half and then gently tap the back of each half with a spoon. Pomegranate juice can stain, so be careful when extracting the seeds. | serves 6

1. Heat the oil in a large saucepan with a lid over medium-high heat and sauté the onion until brown, 5 to 7 minutes. Add the potato, ginger, half the mint, and the green chile and cook, stirring, about 2 minutes.

2. Add the rice and sauté for 3 minutes. Add the water and the salt. Bring to a boil over high heat. Reduce the heat to low, cover the pan, and cook until the rice is done, 10 to 15 minutes. Do not stir the rice while it cooks. Remove from the heat and let rest for about 5 minutes.

3. Transfer to a serving platter and sprinkle with the roasted cumin seeds, pomegranate seeds, and remaining mint leaves before serving.

Gosht ki Dum Biryani

DUM LAMB BIRYANI WITH SAFFRON

Biryani is a popular Indian rice dish made with spices, basmati rice, and meat or vegetables. The spices and condiments used in biryani can vary greatly. *Dum biryani* is a special style made in the South Indian city of Hyderabad. *Dum* refers to the technique of sealing the pot with pastry to keep the moisture in. I cook the meat before combining it with the rice and baking it in a dough-sealed baking dish. It is best served with yogurt or chutney. The deep flavors and piquant aromas of this lamb *biryani* develop very nicely as it slowly cooks in the oven. | serves 4

- 2 cups basmati rice
- 1 1/2 pounds boneless lamb shoulder, cut into 1-inch cubes
- 1 1/2 teaspoons salt, plus more to season lamb
- 2 teaspoons garam masala (page 25)
- 6 tablespoons vegetable oil or ghee
- Two 2-inch-long cinnamon sticks
- 1 teaspoon cumin seeds
- 6 whole cloves
- 5 green cardamom pods
- 2 bay leaves
- 1 teaspoon black peppercorns
- 2 tablespoons minced garlic
- 3 tablespoons peeled, minced fresh ginger
- 3 cups thinly sliced white onion
- 2 teaspoons ground coriander
- 1 1/2 teaspoons ground cumin
- 1/2 teaspoon ground mace
- 1/2 teaspoon freshly grated nutmeg
- 1/2 teaspoon cayenne pepper
- 3 cups water, plus 1 teaspoon for egg wash
- 1 teaspoon saffron, soaked in 1 tablespoon warm water
- 1/3 cup whole milk
- 1 egg white
- One sheet puff pastry, cut into the shape of the baking dish

1. Rinse the rice with cold water to remove the excess starch; drain. Soak the rice in cold water for 30 to 45 minutes. Drain and set aside.

2. Preheat the oven to 325°F. Place the lamb in a large bowl and season it with salt and garam masala. Set aside, covered, for 30 minutes to absorb the flavor of the spices.

3. In a wide, heavy pot, heat the oil or ghee over medium-high heat. Add the lamb and sear in batches until browned on all sides, about 5 minutes. Remove the lamb from the pot and set aside.

4. In the same pot, add the cinnamon, cumin seeds, cloves, cardamom, bay leaves, and black peppercorns and stir until fragrant, about 1 minute. Add the garlic and ginger and stir-fry until aromatic, 2 to 3 minutes. Add the onion and cook, stirring frequently, until very soft, 8 to 10 minutes. Lower the heat, add the coriander, cumin, mace, nutmeg, and cayenne pepper, and stir-fry for an additional minute. Add the lamb and 3 cups water and bring the mixture to a boil. Add the rice and saffron with its soaking water and bring to a boil again. Cook, uncovered, until the water is absorbed by the rice, about 15 minutes. Discard the bay leaves.

continued

5. Transfer the mixture into a 2-quart soufflé dish, and evenly pour the milk over it. Whisk the egg white with 1 teaspoon water and brush the rim of the dish with the egg wash. Gently place the puff pastry directly over the soufflé dish. Press lightly to seal overhanging crust to the sides of the dish. Brush the top surface of the dough with egg wash. Using a fork, poke a few holes in the pastry to allow the steam to vent. Bake for 45 minutes. If the pastry is browning too quickly, cover it with aluminum foil (shiny side out).

6. Remove from the oven and let it stand for 15 minutes before serving.

Khaday Masala Wala Pulao

BASMATI RICE WITH DRY-ROASTED SPICES

- 1 1/2 teaspoons cumin seeds
- 1 teaspoon whole cloves
- 1/2 teaspoon black peppercorns
- 5 to 7 green cardamom pods
- 1 1/2 cups basmati rice, rinsed under cold water several times and drained
- 1 tablespoon vegetable oil or ghee
- 2 3/4 cups water
- 1 1/2 teaspoons salt
- 1 tablespoon finely chopped fresh mint leaves, for garnish

Dry-roasting is a traditional cooking technique for preparing whole spices (see page 17). In this recipe, the spices are first dry-roasted to enhance their flavors, then sautéed in oil, infusing the oil with their flavor, creating a wonderfully fragrant and exotic tasting rice *pulao.* | serves 4

1. Heat a dry, medium saucepan with a lid over medium-high heat. Roast the cumin seeds, cloves, black peppercorns, and cardamom, stirring and shaking the pan, until highly fragrant, about 1 minute. Add the drained rice and oil or ghee and continue to cook another 1 to 3 minutes, stirring gently so as not to break the grains of rice. Add the water and salt and bring to a boil over high heat. Reduce the heat to low, cover the pan, and cook until the rice is done, 10 to 15 minutes. Do not stir the rice while it cooks. Remove from the heat and let rest for 5 minutes.

2. Transfer to a serving platter, garnish with mint, and serve.

Laal Chawal- Subzi Pulao

HIMALAYAN RED RICE VEGETABLE PULAO

- 1 cup Himalayan red rice
- 2 tablespoons unsalted butter
- 1 medium red onion, finely chopped
- 1 teaspoon cumin seeds
- 2 bay leaves
- 4 whole cloves
- 1 tablespoon finely chopped garlic
- 1 medium zucchini, cut into 1-inch cubes
- 1/2 cup fresh or frozen peas, thawed
- 1/2 medium cauliflower, cut into small florets
- 1/2 small carrot, diced
- 2 cups water
- 1 teapoon salt
- 1/2 cup finely chopped fresh cilantro, for garnish

I received a package of Himalayan red rice as a parting gift when I was returning to India after finishing my culinary training in the kitchen of Hotel Soaltee Oberoi in Kathmandu, Nepal. When I cooked it in my kitchen back in Amritsar, everyone was amazed by its deep rosy color and nutty flavor. The Himalayan mountains produce the most aromatic red rice in the world. Red rice takes longer to cook because it has more bran than white rice. Red rice is available in the U.S., mostly in health food stores and gourmet shops. | serves 4

1. Rinse the rice in cold water and drain; soak it in cold water for 15 minutes. Drain and set aside.

2. In a medium pot with a lid, melt the butter over medium heat. Sauté the onion until translucent, about 2 minutes. Add the cumin seeds, bay leaves, cloves, and garlic and stir until very fragrant, about 1 minute. Stir in the zucchini, peas, cauliflower, carrot, and rice. Sauté for a few minutes, stirring, until the rice is well combined. Add the water and salt and bring to a boil. Reduce the heat to low and simmer, covered, until the water is absorbed and the rice is cooked, about 35 minutes. Discard the bay leaves.

3. Fluff the *pulao* with a fork, adjust the salt to taste, and garnish with cilantro before serving.

Kale Chawal aur Matar Pulao

FORBIDDEN RICE & PEAS PULAO

- 1 cup forbidden rice
- 1 1/2 tablespoons olive oil
- 1 teaspoon cumin seeds
- 1 teaspoon black cumin seeds
- 1 medium red onion, finely chopped
- 1 bay leaf
- 2 cloves garlic, minced
- 1/2 cup fresh or frozen peas, thawed
- 1 3/4 cups vegetable stock
- 1 teaspoon salt
- 1/2 teaspoon freshly ground black pepper
- 1 tablespoon garam masala (page 25)

A variation on the usual peas *pulao*, this recipe uses forbidden rice instead of basmati. Forbidden rice is a type of short-grained black rice that turns dark purple when cooked. It has a deep nutty taste. Legend has it that this rice was reserved for the emperors of ancient China. I find it yields a rice dish with great flavor, texture, and color. Forbidden rice can be found in Asian groceries, health food stores, and gourmet shops. | serves 4

1. Rinse the rice with cold water to remove the excess starch; drain. Soak the rice in cold water for 15 minutes. Drain and set aside.

2. Heat the oil over medium heat in a large pot with a lid. Add the cumin seeds, black cumin seeds, onion, bay leaf, and garlic and cook, stirring constantly, until the onion is translucent and the spices become very fragrant, about 5 minutes. Add the rice and peas, stirring to coat rice with oil and lightly toast it, about 1 minute. Stir in the stock and season with salt, pepper, and garam masala. Bring to a boil, cover, and reduce heat to a slow simmer. Cook until rice is tender and liquid is mostly absorbed, 30 to 35 minutes. Adjust salt and pepper to taste, discard the bay leaf, and serve hot.

Palak Paneer wale Chawal

SPINACH & PANEER CHEESE PULAO

Basmati rice *pulao* with spinach and paneer cheese, seasoned with aromatic bay leaf has a great balance of flavors. I serve this tasty and hearty dish with *raita* (page 47). | serves 4 to 6

- 1 1/4 cups basmati rice
- 1 cup vegetable oil
- 8 ounces paneer cheese, cut into 1-inch cubes
- 3 tablespoons ghee or vegetable oil
- 1 dried red hot chile (such as *chile de arbol*), crushed
- 3 bay leaves
- 1 teaspoon black peppercorns
- 2 1/2 cups water
- 1 teaspoon salt
- 4 ounces fresh spinach, chopped

1. Wash and drain the rice and soak it in cold water for 20 minutes. Drain and set aside. Preheat the oven to 250°F.

2. Line a sheet pan with paper towels. Heat the oil in a frying pan on medium heat to 350°F. Test the oil with a cube of cheese: the cheese should begin to bubble immediately. Lightly fry the paneer until golden brown, about 3 minutes. Remove with a slotted spoon and set aside to drain on lined baking sheet.

3. Heat the ghee or oil in a 3 1/2 quart ovenproof pot with a tight lid and fry the red chile, bay leaves, and peppercorns for 1 minute on medium-high heat. Stir in the rice and fry for 2 minutes. Add the water and salt and bring to a boil. Add the cheese, reduce the heat to low, and cover. Simmer for 10 minutes, adding a few tablespoons of water if the rice gets too dry.

4. Stir in the spinach and cook uncovered until the water has evaporated, 5 minutes. Cover with a damp kitchen towel and the lid and place in the oven to bake, 5 minutes.

5. Remove from oven and let stand for 5 minutes. Discard the bay leaves. Adjust salt to taste and serve hot.

Pyaaz- Hari Phool Gobi Pulao

BROWN BASMATI WITH CARAMELIZED ONIONS & BROCCOLI

- 1 1/2 cups brown basmati rice
- 2 3/4 cups water
- 1 teaspoon salt
- 4 tablespoons vegetable oil
- 6 green cardamom pods
- One 1-inch-long piece cinnamon stick
- 6 whole cloves
- 4 small red onions, thinly sliced
- 2 teaspoons sugar
- 1 teaspoon cumin seeds
- 1 teaspoon black mustard seeds
- 1 small head broccoli, cut into 1/2-inch florets
- 1 teaspoon garam masala (page 25)

Brown basmati rice has a mild, nutty flavor, and it's chewier and more nutritious than white rice. Here, it is cooked with broccoli and spices such as cinnamon, cloves, cumin seeds, and mustard seeds, then garnished with caramelized onions. | serves 6

1. Rinse rice under cold running water; drain. Soak the rice in cold water for 1 hour. Drain and set aside.

2. In a saucepan with a lid over high heat, combine the rice, water, and salt and bring to a boil. Reduce the heat to low, cover, and simmer until all the water has been absorbed and the rice is tender, 30 to 35 minutes. Do not stir the rice while it is cooking. Remove from the heat and let rest about 5 minutes.

3. Heat 3 tablespoons oil in a large nonstick saucepan over medium-high heat and cook the cardamom pods, cinnamon, and cloves, stirring, for about 30 seconds. Add the onions; sprinkle the sugar over the onions and cook until brown, stirring as needed, 7 to 8 minutes. Using a slotted spatula, remove half the onions, drain them on paper towels, and reserve for garnish.

4. In a small saucepan with a lid, heat the remaining tablespoon of oil and add the cumin and mustard seeds; they should sputter upon contact with the hot oil. Lower the heat and cover the pan until the sputtering subsides. Quickly add the broccoli florets, garam masala, and the remaining onions and spices and stir for about 2 minutes. Transfer the rice to a serving platter and lightly mix in the broccoli.

5. Serve garnished with the reserved caramelized onions.

Chai Wala Hare Chawal

CHAI-INFUSED EMPEROR'S GREEN RICE

- 1 cup Emperor's green rice, available in Indian groceries
- 2 tablespoons unsalted butter
- 4 bay leaves
- 4 whole cloves
- Two 2-inch-long cinnamon sticks
- 6 green cardamom pods
- One 2-inch-long piece fresh ginger, peeled and minced
- 1 1/2 cups water
- 4 Darjeeling tea bags or any strong black tea (remove the paper tags)
- 1 teaspoon salt
- 1/2 cup finely chopped fresh cilantro, for garnish

When I first bought this dazzling green rice from a specialty store in Los Angeles, I wasn't sure how I was going to cook it. But sometimes the ingredient is so unique that it compels you to create a new recipe around it. This naturally green rice grows in East China around Lake Taihu and maintains its green color after cooking. I combined it with the earthy flavors of chai tea: The chai brings out the nutty flavor of the rice very well. | serves 4

1. Rinse the rice in cold water; drain. Soak it in cold water for 30 minutes. Drain and set aside.

2. Preheat the oven to 350°F. In a medium pot with a lid, melt the butter over medium heat. Add the bay leaves, cloves, cinnamon, cardamom, and ginger and stir until very fragrant, about 2 minutes. Add the rice and sauté for a few minutes until the rice and spices are well combined. Add the water, tea bags, and salt and bring to a boil. Cover with a damp kitchen towel and a lid and bake for 12 to 15 minutes, or until the liquid is evaporated. Remove the tea bags carefully, without tearing them open.

3. Fluff with a fork and garnish with cilantro.

BREAD

In northern India, bread is so important that when my grandmother used to ask me if I was hungry, she didn't ask me if I wanted to eat food, she asked if I wanted to eat *roti*. Where I'm from, *roti* is synonymous with food.

• • •

If you're having dinner in an Indian home, your plate will always have a piece of bread on it, whether it's *roti*, *poori*, or *parathas*. Most Indian breads are made fresh, but they can also be premade and reheated in an oven.

CAROM SEEDS POORI

MINT AND CUMIN SEEDS POORI

FRESH CILANTRO, GINGER AND CURRY LEAF DOSAS

SOUTH INDIAN–STYLE RICE PANCAKE

NAAN

GARLIC AND CILANTRO NAAN

MISSI ROTI WITH FRESH CILANTRO

SPINACH AND BASIL ROTI

MULTI-LAYERED WHOLE WHEAT PARATHAS

Ajwain wali Poori

CAROM SEEDS POORI

Pooris are Indian fried flatbreads regularly served at festivals and celebrations. They are usually made with whole-wheat flour. This recipe calls for carom seeds for added flavor and offers tips to achieve a puffed bread. | makes 8 *pooris*

1 cup whole-wheat flour

1/2 cup all-purpose flour, plus more for dusting

1/4 teaspoon carom seeds, coarsely ground

1/4 teaspoon salt

3 tablespoons vegetable oil, plus more for bowl and deep-frying

1/3 to 1/2 cup water

1. In a food processor or by hand, mix together all the dry ingredients and then add in the vegetable oil, followed by 1/3 cup water, mixing until a smooth, satiny, firm dough is formed. Add more water if needed. Firmer dough helps make the *poori* puff up better and also absorbs less oil when frying.

2. Turn the dough onto a floured work surface and knead for 5 minutes. Place in an oiled bowl. Cover with plastic wrap and let rest for 30 minutes.

3. Divide the dough into 8 equal portions and roll into balls. Apply oil on opposite sides of the dough balls and flatten each with a rolling pin into a round disk 3 to 4 inches in diameter.

4. Line a sheet pan with paper towels. Fill a medium saucepan or heavy-bottom pan a third full with canola oil, about 4 inches, and set it over medium-high heat; heat to 350°F. Test the oil by dropping in a small piece of dough. The oil is ready if the dough sizzles upon contact and begins to brown within a minute. Deep-fry the bread, one at the time, until golden brown, 3 to 4 minutes, turning once to ensure it puffs up. Pressing the dough down gently beneath the surface of the oil with a slotted spoon while the *poori* is frying helps to make it puff up. Place *pooris* on lined sheet pan to drain and serve immediately.

Pudinay our Jeera wali Poori

VARIATION: MINT & CUMIN SEEDS POORI

Make as directed above, substituting 10 fresh mint leaves, minced, 1 tablespoon dried mint leaves, and 1/4 teaspoon cumin seeds, coarsely ground for the carom seeds.

Rava Dosa

FRESH CILANTRO, GINGER & CURRY LEAF DOSAS

- 2 cups semolina flour
- 2 tablespoons rice flour
- 1 cup plain, lowfat yogurt
- 2 tablespoons finely chopped fresh cilantro
- One 2-inch-long piece fresh ginger, peeled and minced
- 5 to 6 fresh curry leaves, coarsely chopped
- 1 teaspoon salt
- 2 cups warm water
- Vegetable oil cooking spray
- 3 tablespoons vegetable oil

Rava dosas, as they're called in India, are made of semolina (*rava* means semolina), and are delicious on their own or with vegetables, lentils, or an assortment of chutneys. Typically a South Indian dish, *dosas* are also made with gram (chickpea) flour and are similar to *socca*, a popular street snack in Nice, France. | serves 4 to 6

1. In a medium bowl combine the semolina flour, rice flour, yogurt, cilantro, ginger, curry leaves, and salt. Stir in the water a little at a time; continue to stir until the batter is smooth. Cover the bowl and let the batter rest for about 1 hour.

2. Heat a large griddle or a flat, nonstick pan over medium-high heat. Spray a little cooking spray on the griddle. Pour 1/2 cup batter on the griddle, moving in a circle out from the middle, trying to distribute the batter in as large a circle as possible. Immediately use the back of a wooden spoon or a rubber spatula to spread the batter to cover any gaps in the middle, trying to increase the diameter of the crêpe to 8 or 9 inches. Drizzle a few drops of vegetable oil over the crêpe as it cooks. Cook until golden brown on the bottom, 3 to 4 minutes. Loosen it from the griddle with a sharp-edged spatula and flip it; cook for another minute. Repeat with the remaining batter, cleaning the griddle with a dry kitchen towel and lightly spraying the griddle with oil between each batch. Serve immediately, before they lose their crispy texture.

Chawal ki Roti

SOUTH INDIAN-STYLE RICE PANCAKE

- 1 cup basmati rice
- 1/2 cup white lentils (available at south Asian groceries)
- 1 teaspoon salt
- 1 teaspoon sugar
- 1/2 teaspoon baking soda
- 5 tablespoons ghee or vegetable oil

This delicious rice pancake is eaten as a snack all day long and is a favorite dish of South India. You can add your favorite vegetables or finely shredded cooked meats for a topping or serve with chutney. | serves 4 to 6

1. In a large mixing bowl combine the rice and lentils and rinse them under cold running water until the water runs clear. Cover with water by about 4 inches and let them soak for at least 2 hours.

2. Drain the lentils and rice and place them in a blender; grind to a smooth paste. Add a little water if necessary to form a thick batter.

3. Add the salt, sugar, and baking soda to the batter and mix well. Set aside at room temperature for 4 to 5 hours.

4. Heat a griddle or nonstick pan over medium-high heat and brush it with a little ghee or oil. Pour on 2 to 3 tablespoons of batter, spreading it evenly with the back of a spoon into a thick circle about 4 inches in diameter. Drizzle a little ghee on top of the pancake. Cook until small bubbles appear on the surface, about 5 minutes. Turn over and cook the other side until crisp and golden, another 2 minutes. Reoil the griddle after each pancake. Serve hot with your favorite chutney.

Naan

NAAN

This is a great recipe for authentic make-at-home naan, a soft Indian flatbread. I like serving it with a light brushing of ghee or butter. If you don't have a baking stone, a cast-iron skillet can do the job. Preheat the skillet on the stove top then put it in the oven, bottom side up for the naan to cook upon. Naan baked in a conventional oven puffs up more than naan baked in the traditional tandoor. | makes 6 naan

1 teaspoon active dry yeast

1/2 teaspoon sugar

1/3 cup warm water (about 110°F)

1 cup all-purpose flour, plus more as needed while kneading

1/2 teaspoon salt

2 medium eggs, lightly beaten

2 tablespoons plain, lowfat yogurt

1/4 cup plus 1 teaspoon ghee or vegetable oil

1. In a glass measuring cup, combine the yeast and sugar. Add the water and stir well. Let rest until foamy, about 5 minutes.

2. Sift the flour and salt together into a large bowl. Make a well in the center of the flour and pour in the yeast mixture, eggs, yogurt, and 1/4 cup ghee or oil. Mix together with your fingers until a smooth dough forms, working in a small amount of additional flour if needed. Knead for 3 minutes.

3. Oil a small bowl with the remaining 1 teaspoon ghee or oil. Place the dough in the bowl, turning to coat; cover with plastic wrap and let rest in a warm place until doubled in size, about 1 hour.

4. Place a baking stone in the bottom of the oven and preheat oven to 400°F. Divide the dough into 6 pieces and gently roll into balls. Gently roll each ball into a 6-inch circle on a lightly floured surface. Bake dough on the baking stone in batches until just golden brown and puffed, 8 to 10 minutes. You should be able to bake two naan at a time on an average-size baking stone. Serve immediately.

Lassan-Dhaniya ka Naan

VARIATION: GARLIC & CILANTRO NAAN

Make as directed above, gently rolling the balls of dough into 6-inch circles. Brush each circle with ghee or oil (about 2 teaspoons total) and top evenly with 1/4 cup finely chopped fresh cilantro and 4 cloves of garlic, finely chopped. Gently press the cilantro and garlic into the dough so they adhere. Continue baking as directed.

I've Only Just Begun

The highlight of my days continued to be Biji teaching me to cook. I was twelve years old when Biji first entrusted me with making the yellow lentils for the evening family meal. She didn't tell anyone I had made the lentils and when they accepted them as if they were Biji's, I was hooked on cooking.

It takes many years to understand the intricacies of the spices used in Indian cooking. The interplay of the whole and ground spices with herbs requires a good deal of practice to get just right. Through Biji's lessons, I gradually began to develop this knowledge. Yet, her utter ease in the kitchen may have made me overly confident in my own abilities.

On one hot summer day, Biji was in bed with a fever and unable to prepare dinner. With foolish overconfidence, I courageously took on the important task of cooking the evening meal on my own. I still remember how hot it was as I tried to finish everything before my family woke up from their naps. I was so anxious to get the job done that most of the food was raw and none of the spices had been properly handled. It was a disaster. Everyone was unhappy with me; even the yellow lentils I thought I had mastered went wrong.

Biji got up from bed to find me surrounded by the glaring family. I stood there helplessly looking to my Biji for encouragement, blinking quickly, trying to keep the tears in. With her croaking voice she said, "When I cooked my first meal, I added sugar instead of salt in everything." I looked into her loving eyes and I knew that I had not failed, but only just begun. Since that day, I have never let failure slow me down.

Dhaniya wali Missi Roti

MISSI ROTI WITH FRESH CILANTRO

Missi roti, a favorite crisp bread of the Punjab and Rajasthan states in Northern India, is made with gram (chickpea) and whole-wheat flours. A staple ingredient in Indian cuisine, gram flour lends a slightly nutty flavor to many dishes. I add pomegranate seeds to the dough for a sweet, tart crunch. This *roti* is great hot off the griddle. | makes 12 *rotis*

- 3 cups gram (chickpea) flour
- 1 cup whole-wheat flour
- 1 small red onion, finely chopped
- 2 fresh green chile peppers (such as serrano), seeded and finely chopped
- 1 teaspoon dried pomegranate seeds
- 1 tablespoon ghee or vegetable oil, plus extra for frying
- 2 tablespoons plain, lowfat yogurt
- 3 tablespoons finely chopped fresh cilantro
- 1 1/3 cups warm water
- All-purpose flour, for dusting

1. In a large mixing bowl, combine the flours, onion, green chiles, pomegranate seeds, 1 tablespoon ghee or oil, yogurt, cilantro, and warm water to form a stiff dough. Knead well until smooth, adding a little more water if necessary.

2. Divide the dough into 12 portions; roll into balls. On a lightly floured work surface, roll the balls into 5 to 6 inch disks.

3. Heat a frying pan or a griddle over high heat. Add about 1/2 teaspoon ghee or oil. When the oil is hot, place a disk on it. Cook until the dough browns slightly and dark bubbles form beneath the surface, about 1 minute. Flip the *roti* with a spatula and cook the other side, about 1 minute. Lightly brush each side with ghee or oil and repeat flipping until it is evenly cooked. Wipe down the pan and reoil after each *roti*. Serve immediately.

Palak-Tulsi Roti

SPINACH & BASIL ROTI

- 4 cups fresh spinach leaves, chopped
- 4 cups (1 pound) whole-wheat flour, plus more for dusting
- 1 teaspoon salt
- 1 cup fresh basil leaves, chopped
- 1 teaspoon vegetable oil, plus more for bowl and griddle
- 1 to 1 1/4 cups water
- 1/4 cup ghee, at room temperature

Growing up, we made *roti* everyday at home using whole-wheat flour. In this recipe, I have added spinach and basil to give the flatbreads a fresh, earthy flavor. | makes 20 *rotis*

1. In a medium pan over medium-high heat, briefly wilt the spinach until soft. Let cool, then wring dry in a kitchen towel.

2. Sift the flour and salt into a bowl and make a well in the center. Add the spinach, basil, oil, and water to the well and mix, folding in the flour, to form a soft dough. Turn out the dough onto a floured surface and knead for 5 minutes, adding a little more water if needed. Place in an oiled bowl, cover with a damp kitchen towel, and let rest for 30 minutes.

3. Divide the dough into 20 portions; roll into balls. On a lightly floured surface, evenly roll each ball out into a very thin 6-inch circle.

4. Heat a flat griddle over medium-high heat, oil it lightly, and cook the *roti* one at a time until brown around the edges, 2 to 3 minutes on each side. Reoil the griddle after each *roti*.

5. Brush lightly with ghee and serve warm.

Khasta Paratha

MULTI-LAYERED WHOLE-WHEAT PARATHAS

As a child, I looked forward to our special weekend breakfasts when I could eat *parathas*, crispy and flaky on the outside and chewy inside. *Parathas* are my comfort food, and even now I still try to make them fresh for breakfast every Sunday with mint-flavored yogurt or a pickle. | makes 12 *parathas*

- 2 cups whole-wheat flour, plus more for dusting
- 1 cup all-purpose flour
- 1 teaspoon salt
- 1/2 cup warm water
- 1/2 cup whole milk
- 1/2 cup vegetable oil or ghee

1. Sift the flours and the salt together. Add the water, milk, and 1 tablespoon oil or ghee and knead to make a dough. Oil a small bowl with 1 teaspoon oil, place the dough into the bowl, turning to coat, cover with plastic wrap, and let rest for about 30 minutes.

2. Divide the dough into 12 equal portions and roll them into balls. Roll a ball out into a 6-inch disk on a lightly floured work surface, brush the disk with oil or ghee, and lightly dust with flour. Roll the disk up to form a long tube. Place the tube of dough on the lightly floured work surface and coil it into a tight circle. Flatten it with the palm of your hand and roll it out again to a 6-inch disk. This technique of creating folds in the dough is what makes the *paratha* layered after cooking. Repeat with the remaining dough balls.

3. Lightly oil a frying pan or a griddle and preheat the pan over high. Once hot, place a disk of dough on the pan and immediately turn the heat down slightly to medium-high (turn it back up for each successive *paratha*). Cook until the dough browns slightly and dark bubbles form beneath the surface, about 1 minute. Flip the *paratha* over with a spatula and cook the other side, 1 minute. After each side has browned, lightly brush the sides with oil or ghee and repeat flipping until the *paratha* is evenly cooked, about 2 more minutes. Wipe down the griddle with a kitchen towel and reoil the pan before cooking each *paratha*. Serve immediately.

LEGUMES

Legumes are comfort food for many Indians. They are easy to grow and store, cheap to buy, and simple to prepare. Their great variety of colors, flavors, and textures is one of the many reasons that vegetarians are drawn to Indian cuisine.

. . .

These recipes will show you how to create tasty vegetarian dishes with a variety of legumes and vegetables. Once you're familiar with the recipes, feel free to substitute other beans and lentils you have on hand. These dishes are perfect served over rice or just on their own with your favorite bread.

- 1 1/2 cups dried black chickpeas, rinsed, soaked in cold water overnight, and drained
- 2 quarts water
- 1/4 teaspoon salt
- 3 tablespoons ghee
- 1 tablespoon cumin seeds
- 10 fresh curry leaves
- 2 medium red onions, chopped
- 1 tablespoon peeled, minced fresh ginger
- 3 fresh green chile peppers (such as serrano), minced
- 1 cup finely chopped tomatoes
- 5 scallions, finely chopped
- 1 tablespoon ground coriander
- 1/2 teaspoon dark red chile powder, preferably ancho
- 1 tablespoon garam masala (page 25)
- 1/4 cup chopped fresh cilantro, for garnish
- 1 small red onion, thinly sliced, for garnish
- 4 lime wedges, for garnish

Ghar Jaisi Daal

HOME-STYLE DRY BENGAL GRAM

Bengal gram, or *kala channa* as it is known as in India, is a black variety of chickpea. The beans are dark and small with a rough coat. They are sold whole (as opposed to split) and have a particularly savory flavor. Bengal gram is cultivated mainly in the Indian subcontinent and served in temples during important Hindu religious ceremonies. Recipes for dry Bengal gram (dry because the chickpeas aren't cooked in sauce) can vary but this is how I remember it always being cooked in my house. If you can't find Bengal gram, regular chickpeas can be substituted. | serves 4

1. In a large saucepan with a lid over high heat, combine the black chickpeas, water, and salt. Bring to a boil. Reduce the heat to low, cover partially, and simmer until the chickpeas are tender, 45 to 60 minutes. Drain and set aside.

2. In a large saucepan, heat the ghee over medium-high heat and add the cumin seeds; they should sizzle upon contact with the hot oil. Add the curry leaves and chopped onions and cook until dark golden-brown, stirring frequently to prevent sticking. Add the ginger, green chiles, tomatoes, and scallions and cook for 3 to 5 minutes. Mix in the coriander, chile powder, and garam masala. Add the chickpeas and cook over high heat until all the liquid evaporates and the chickpeas are glazed with a dark brown coating, 10 to 15 minutes.

3. Serve garnished with fresh cilantro, sliced red onion, and lime wedges.

Malai Lobiya

CREAMY BLACK-EYED PEAS WITH CASHEW SAUCE

- 1 cup dried black-eyed peas
- 12 cups water
- Salt
- 1/4 cup ghee
- 1 small onion, finely chopped
- 4 green cardamom pods
- 3 cloves garlic, minced
- One 2-inch-long piece fresh ginger, peeled and finely chopped
- 1/4 cup finely ground cashews
- 1 cup heavy cream
- 2 tablespoons finely chopped fresh cilantro

A friend of mine gave me this recipe years ago and it was a welcome change from the usual curried black-eyed peas that I was used to having at home. The cashew sauce is rich and creamy and goes well with the smooth texture of the beans. Black-eyed peas cook fast and do not need to soak in advance. | serves 4

1. Place the peas in a large pot with a lid, add the water and a generous pinch of salt, and bring water to a boil over high heat. Reduce the heat to medium-low, cover, and simmer until the peas are tender, about 20 minutes. Drain and reserve the peas.

2. Meanwhile, heat the ghee in a large saucepan over medium-high heat and add the onion, cardamom, garlic, and ginger; fry until the spices darken slightly and are fragrant and the onion begins to caramelize, about 5 minutes. Stir in the black-eyed peas, cashews, cream, and cilantro and cook until thick and well combined, 8 to 10 minutes. Adjust the seasoning with salt to taste and serve hot.

Ghiya aur Hari Moong Daal

SQUASH & GREEN LENTIL MEDLEY

Green lentils, summer squash, and a variety of spices make a colorful accompaniment to breads and rice. The delicate flavor, soft shell, and creamy white flesh of summer squash is a perfect addition to any summer meal. I make sure that the squash I select is ripe and firm. Green lentils are known for their earthy flavor and are delicious as well as nutritious. | serves 4

- 1 cup dried green lentils, picked over, washed, and drained
- 1/2 teaspoon ground turmeric
- Salt
- 1/4 cup vegetable oil
- 1 teaspoon cumin seeds
- 2 whole star anise
- 1 small onion, finely chopped
- 2 cloves garlic, minced
- 3 medium summer squashes, cut into 1-inch cubes
- 1 teaspoon ground cumin
- 1 teaspoon ground coriander
- 1/2 cup water
- Juice of 1 lemon
- 2 tablespoons finely chopped fresh cilantro

1. Place the lentils, turmeric, and a pinch of salt in a large pot, cover with water by 2 inches, and bring to a boil over high heat, skimming off any foam. Reduce the heat to low and simmer until the lentils are cooked but still firm, 20 to 25 minutes. Drain and reserve the lentils.

2. Meanwhile, heat the oil in a medium saucepan over medium heat. Add the cumin seeds and star anise and fry until slightly darkened and fragrant, about 2 minutes. Add the onion and garlic and cook, stirring until golden brown, about 5 minutes. Stir in the squash, ground cumin, and coriander and cook for 2 minutes, stirring until well combined. Add water and cook until the squash is cooked, about 5 minutes. Stir in the lentils, lemon juice, and cilantro and cook until well combined. Adjust the seasoning with salt to taste and serve hot.

Ravivaar Rajma

SUNDAY KIDNEY BEAN & TOMATO CURRY

Throughout my childhood, we looked forward to Sunday lunch, when my grandmother would bring out the pot of red bean curry and plain basmati rice. When I sit down to a pot of these beans, I feel that all is right with the world. Over the years, even though I have come up with my own version of the beans, the main flavor of those Sunday afternoons remains the same. Easy and quick to make, this dish tastes as if a lot of work went into it—perfect for a Sunday when you want to relax and eat well. Serve with Okra Raita (page 47). | serves 4

- 2 tablespoons vegetable oil
- 1 teaspoon cumin seeds
- 2 medium red onions, finely chopped
- 1 1/2 teaspoons chopped fresh thyme
- 2 teaspoons peeled, minced fresh ginger
- 4 cloves garlic, minced
- 2 fresh green chile peppers (such as serrano), minced
- 2 large plum tomatoes, chopped
- 2 teaspoons ground coriander
- 1 teaspoon ground cumin
- 1/4 teaspoon ground turmeric
- 1 teaspoon garam masala (page 25)
- 1 (15 1/2-ounce) can kidney beans, rinsed and drained
- 2 cups water
- 1/2 teaspoon salt
- 2 sprigs fresh cilantro, for garnish

1. In a large saucepan, heat the oil over medium-high heat; add the cumin seeds and let sizzle for 1 minute. Add the onions and thyme and cook, stirring frequently, until the onions begin to brown, about 5 minutes. Add the ginger, garlic, green chiles, tomatoes, coriander, cumin, turmeric, and garam masala and fry until very fragrant, 4 to 5 minutes.

2. To the same saucepan, add the beans, water, and salt and cook until the flavors are well developed, about 10 minutes.

3. Reduce heat to low. Remove about 1/2 cup beans, mash them, and add back to the pot. Mix well. Simmer until sauce thickens, about 10 minutes. Adjust the salt to taste.

4. Transfer to a serving bowl and serve garnished with a few sprigs of cilantro.

Comfort Daal

RED LENTILS WITH CILANTRO & MINT

Indian *dal*, a traditional rich and hearty lentil curry, is made with red lentils, which have a tendency to cook quickly. The touch of mint adds a nice fragrance, and the spices and lemon juice provide a tangy flavor. | serves 4

- 1 cup dried red lentils, picked over, washed, and drained
- 1/4 teaspoon ground turmeric
- 1 bay leaf
- Pinch of salt
- 2 tablespoons vegetable oil
- 1 small red onion, finely chopped
- 1/2 tablespoon peeled, minced fresh ginger
- 1/2 tablespoon minced garlic
- 1 fresh green chile pepper (such as serrano), minced, with seeds
- 1 tablespoon ground coriander
- 1/2 teaspoon ground cumin
- 1/4 teaspoon ground cinnamon
- 1/4 teaspoon paprika
- 1 teaspoon sugar
- 3 tablespoons finely chopped fresh cilantro, plus 1 tablespoon for garnish
- 3 tablespoons finely chopped fresh mint leaves
- 2 tablespoons fresh lemon juice

1. In a saucepan over high heat, combine the lentils, turmeric, bay leaf, and salt. Cover with water by 2 inches and bring to a boil. Reduce the heat to medium and simmer, uncovered, stirring occasionally, until the lentils are tender but still firm, 12 to 15 minutes. Drain and set aside.

2. In a small frying pan, heat the oil over medium heat. Add the onion, ginger, garlic, green chile, coriander, cumin, cinnamon, paprika, and sugar. Reduce the heat to low and cook until fragrant, about 2 minutes. Remove from heat. Discard the bay leaf.

3. In a large bowl, combine the lentils and the spice mixture, tossing gently to mix. Stir in the cilantro and mint, then stir in the lemon juice. Serve garnished with freshly chopped cilantro.

Safed Rajma Curry

CANNELLINI BEANS WITH MADRAS CURRY POWDER

Though most curry powders are more aromatic than intensely spicy, Madras curry powder has a hot kick with a deep red color to match. Cumin is added to give the vegetable oil an intense flavor. | serves 4

- 1 cup dried cannellini beans, rinsed, soaked overnight, and drained
- 6 1/2 cups water
- 1 teaspoon salt
- 2 bay leaves
- One 1-inch-long piece cinnamon stick
- 3 tablespoons vegetable oil
- 1 clove garlic, minced
- 1 1/2 teaspoons cumin seeds
- 2 large tomatoes, finely chopped
- 2 fresh green chile peppers (such as serrano), minced
- 1 1/2 tablespoons peeled, minced fresh ginger
- 2 tablespoons Madras curry powder (page 23)
- 2 tablespoons ground coriander
- 1 teaspoon ground cumin
- 1/2 teaspoon ground turmeric
- 1/2 cup plain, lowfat yogurt, whisked smooth
- 1/2 cup finely chopped fresh cilantro
- 1/4 teaspoon garam masala (page 25)

1. In a large saucepan over high heat, combine the beans, 6 cups water, salt, bay leaves, and cinnamon. Bring to a boil. Reduce the heat to low and continue to simmer until the beans are tender, 50 minutes to an hour. Drain the water and reserve the beans.

2. In a large saucepan, heat the oil over medium-high heat and cook the garlic until golden, about 1 minute. Add the cumin seeds; they should sizzle upon contact with the hot oil, cook for 1 minute, stirring constantly. Add the tomatoes, green chiles, and ginger and cook, stirring constantly, initially over high and then over medium heat until all the juices evaporate, about 10 minutes. Add the curry powder, coriander, ground cumin, and turmeric and cook, stirring, 1 minute. Then add the yogurt, a little at a time until it is absorbed, stirring constantly to prevent it from curdling. Mix in the beans and cilantro. Add 1/2 cup water and simmer for another 10 to 15 minutes, uncovered. Discard the bay leaves.

3. Transfer to a serving dish and sprinkle with the garam masala.

Punjabi Choley

PUNJAB-STYLE CHICKPEAS MASALA

1 tablespoon ground dried pomegranate seeds
2 teaspoons ground cumin
1 teaspoon mango powder
1/2 teaspoon garam masala (page 25)
1/2 teaspoon cayenne pepper
3 tablespoons vegetable oil
1 tablespoon peeled, minced fresh ginger
2 tablespoons minced garlic
2 fresh green chile peppers (such as serrano), minced
1 tablespoon ground coriander
1 (15 1/2-ounce) can chickpeas, drained and rinsed well
Pinch of salt
1/2 cup water
1 teaspoon cumin seeds
One 1-inch-long piece fresh ginger, peeled and cut into thin matchsticks
1 small red onion, sliced
2 small tomatoes, diced
1/2 cup chopped fresh cilantro, for garnish

This is an important comfort food recipe and a classic North Indian vegetarian dish. I like serving it with warm crispy *poori*. The spiciness in this recipe can be adjusted to suit your palate. To save time, I use canned chickpeas, but you can use dried chickpeas, soaked overnight and cooked in the same way as the chickpeas in Home-Style Dry Bengal Gram (page 112). | serves 4

1. Place the ground pomegranate seeds, cumin, mango powder, garam masala, and cayenne pepper in a small skillet and toast over medium heat, stirring constantly until fragrant and slightly brown, about 1 minute. Transfer to a small bowl and set aside.

2. Heat 2 tablespoons of vegetable oil in a large saucepan over medium-high heat and add the ginger, garlic, and green chiles, stirring until golden, about 1 minute. Add the coriander and mix in the chickpeas, salt, and water and cook, stirring as needed, until the pan is almost dry, about 5 minutes. Add the roasted spices, reduce the heat to medium, and cook another 5 minutes. Transfer to a serving dish and keep warm.

3. Heat the remaining 1 tablespoon oil in a small saucepan over medium-high heat and add the cumin seeds; they should sizzle on contact. Quickly add the ginger matchsticks, onion, and tomatoes and cook, stirring, until golden, about 1 minute.

4. Place the chickpeas in a serving bowl and top with the onion and tomato mixture. Serve hot, garnished with cilantro.

The Secrets of Goat Biryani

On many Sundays growing up, my family visited my father's friend Ramesh, who was more like an uncle to us. We spent those beautiful days flying kites on his terrace and eating goat *biryani.* To spend more time in the kitchen with Biji and the other women in the family who cooked with her, I'd make up excuses to my cousins, telling them I was scared of heights. Once I got to the kitchen, I always received the same reaction: "The kitchen is for women! Get out!" I would hear laughter as I left, feeling just a little bit disheartened, but never fully deterred.

I kept going back to the kitchen and gradually the women stopped noticing me. I stayed out of the way and learned by watching. In order to have more time in the kitchen to talk amongst themselves, Biji and the other women pretended that many of the dishes were much more intricate and difficult to prepare than they really were. I realized that this was food I already knew, just made with slightly different ingredients (Uncle Ramesh had more money for food than my family).

The fact that it was the same food I always ate, goat *biryani* for example, but just more complex, stirred my imagination. I spent my days dreaming up all kinds of foods—different sauces and combinations that I "cooked" with only my imagination. I was taught that Indian cuisine had many rules developed over the centuries—there was one "right way" of making a dish, and you were not supposed to deviate or create something new. I still had much to learn about food, but I began to realize that one day I'd be able to express my culinary creativity. But first, the time-honored secrets of goat *biryani* and many other dishes had to become mine.

Daal Subz

BROWN LENTILS & ZUCCHINI WITH LIME

- 1 1/2 cups dried brown lentils, picked over, washed, and drained
- 1/2 teaspoon ground turmeric
- Pinch of salt
- 4 tablespoons vegetable oil
- 1 teaspoon black mustard seeds
- 1 small onion, finely chopped
- 3 medium zucchini, cut into 1-inch cubes
- 1/3 cup water
- 1 fresh green chile pepper (such as serrano), minced
- 1 teaspoon *chaat masala* (page 20)
- Juice of 1 lime

Both healthy and tasty, this is one of my favorite dishes. Brown lentils become soft and mushy if overcooked, so a little more care than usual is needed in their preparation. Adding oil to the cooking water helps keep them firm. *Chaat masala* adds a tangy note to round out the dish. | serves 4 to 6

1. Place the lentils, turmeric, and salt in a large pot, cover with water by 2 inches, and bring to a boil over high heat, skimming off any foam. Reduce the heat to low, add 2 tablespoons of oil, and simmer until the lentils are cooked and still firm, about 20 minutes. Drain and reserve the lentils.

2. Meanwhile, heat the remaining 2 tablespoons oil in a medium saucepan over medium heat. Add the mustard seeds and fry until they start to crackle, about 2 minutes. Add the onion and cook, stirring, until golden brown, 5 minutes. Stir in the zucchini and cook for 2 minutes, stirring until well combined. Add about 1/3 cup water and cook until the liquid is evaporated and the zucchini is cooked, about 3 minutes. You may need to turn the heat to high if the zucchini finishes cooking well before the water evaporates. Stir in the lentils, green chile, *chaat masala*, and lime juice and cook until well combined, about 5 minutes.

- 1 1/2 cups dried black chickpeas, rinsed, soaked in cold water overnight, and drained
- Pinch of salt, plus 1 teaspoon
- 3 tablespoons vegetable oil
- 1 tablespoon peeled, minced fresh ginger
- 2 tablespoons minced garlic
- 2 fresh green chile peppers (such as serrano), minced
- 2 teaspoons ground cumin
- 1 teaspoon mango powder
- 1/2 teaspoon garam masala (page 25)
- 1/2 teaspoon cayenne pepper
- 1 tablespoon ground coriander
- 2 medium red onions, chopped
- 1 small tomato, diced
- 2 tablespoons honey
- Juice of 1 lemon
- 1/2 cup chopped fresh cilantro

Kala Channa aur Shahad ki Chaat

BLACK CHICKPEA CHAAT WITH SPICY HONEY DRESSING

Chaat, an Indian word meaning "to taste," is the name of a popular type of street food in India. Made from readily available ingredients, these dishes are mixed together quickly and highly seasoned. This recipe combines black chickpeas (Bengal gram) and spices and is often served over potato cakes (page 66). My grandfather and I enjoyed a snack like this when he took me on a pilgrimage to the Vaishno Devi temple in northern India. We hiked for many miles and were glad to have these chickpeas for a snack on the way. | serves 4 to 6

1. In a large saucepan with a lid over high heat, combine the chickpeas and a pinch of salt, cover with water by 2 inches, and bring to a boil. Reduce the heat to low, cover partially, and simmer until the chickpeas are tender, about 45 minutes. Drain and set aside.

2. Heat the oil in a large saucepan with a lid over medium-high heat and add the ginger, garlic, and green chiles, stirring until golden, about 1 minute. Add the chickpeas, cumin, mango powder, garam masala, cayenne pepper, coriander, and 1 teaspoon salt and mix well for about 1 minute. Add the onions, tomato, honey, lemon juice, and cilantro and toss to combine; cook, stirring, until dry, about 2 minutes. Serve hot.

Haldi- Adrak wali Peeli Daal

YELLOW LENTILS WITH TURMERIC & GINGER

As best as I can remember, I was eleven years old when my grandmother, Biji, taught me how to make *dal*, a staple dish in many Indian households. Growing up, we ate *dal* with most meals. Biji waited until my family had enjoyed the *dal* a few times before revealing that I was the cook. No one could deny I had made it well. *Dal* is the simplest way to prepare lentils. I love the smooth, warm taste of ginger here. | serves 4

- 1 cup dried yellow lentils, picked over, washed, and drained
- 1 teaspoon ground turmeric
- Salt
- 2 tablespoons ghee or vegetable oil
- 1 tablespoon cumin seeds, plus 1 teaspoon dry-roasted (see page 17) and coarsely ground
- 1 medium white onion, finely chopped
- 1 tablespoon finely chopped garlic
- One 1-inch-long piece fresh ginger, peeled and finely chopped
- 1 fresh green chile pepper (such as serrano), seeded and minced
- 3 tablespoons chopped fresh cilantro
- Basmati rice (page 78) or bread, for serving

1. Combine the lentils, turmeric, and a pinch of salt in a medium saucepan, cover with water by 2 inches, and bring to a boil over high heat. Skim froth from the surface continuously while boiling for the first 5 minutes. Reduce the heat to low and simmer, uncovered, until the lentils are tender and cooked, about 30 minutes. Leave over low heat to keep the lentils warm until ready to use.

2. In a medium skillet, heat the ghee or oil over medium-high heat and add the cumin seeds. Cook, stirring, until slightly darker and fragrant, about 2 minutes. Add the onion, garlic, ginger, and green chile and cook, stirring, until the onion is translucent and the garlic begins to brown, about 3 minutes. Stir in the lentils and cilantro and cook until well combined, about 5 minutes. Season with salt to taste and sprinkle with dry-roasted ground cumin.

3. Serve hot with rice or bread.

SOUPS & SALADS

When it comes to soups and salads, there's never an off-season; they can be easily customized to highlight seasonal ingredients. Soups are a great way to showcase the warmth and comfort of Indian home cooking. From thick and creamy to light and herbaceous, these recipes go far beyond just mulligatawny.

...

With the season's best produce at hand, salads provide the perfect way to experiment with new flavor combinations. Spice-infused oils and dressings provide an unexpected pop, while letting the bright, fresh vegetables and fruit shine.

CREAM OF TOMATO SOUP WITH GARLIC CROUTONS

GINGER AND CURRY LEAF RASAM

SPRING ONION AND PEA SOUP

CUMIN-SCENTED CREAM OF SPINACH SOUP

GUJARATI YOGURT AND COCONUT SOUP

FISHERMAN'S SOUP WITH SAGE

SPINACH AND WALNUT SALAD WITH CURRY DRESSING

SOYBEAN SPROUT AND PERSIMMON SALAD

FRENCH BREAKFAST RADISHES
WITH MUSTARD SEED DRESSING

SUMMER CUCUMBER SALAD WITH LEMON DRESSING

TANGY FRUIT SALAD

PEA AND YAM SALAD

Tamatar ka Shorba

CREAM OF TOMATO SOUP WITH GARLIC CROUTONS

Personally, I prefer a rich, creamy tomato soup over a water-based version. In this recipe, cooked tomatoes are puréed with cardamom and cinnamon. For a lighter soup, replace the cream with half-and-half. Sun-dried tomatoes, if added, impart a wonderful texture. | serves 4

FOR THE SOUP:

- 1 pound ripe tomatoes, coarsely chopped
- 1 medium potato (such as Idaho), peeled and chopped
- 1 medium red onion, chopped
- 2 tablespoons tomato paste or 4 sundried tomatoes, soaked in warm water for 10 minutes
- 4 green cardamom pods
- One 1-inch-long piece cinnamon stick
- 4 cups vegetable stock
- 1 teaspoon salt
- 1 cup heavy cream
- 2 tablespoons chopped fresh cilantro, for garnish

FOR THE CROUTONS:

- 1 tablespoon butter
- 1 tablespoon chopped garlic
- 2 slices Italian white bread, cut into 1/2-inch cubes

1. Make the soup: In a large pot with a lid bring the tomatoes, potato, onion, tomato paste or sundried tomatoes, cardamom, cinnamon, vegetable stock, and salt to a boil. Reduce the heat, cover, and simmer until the potatoes are cooked through, about 20 minutes. Let cool for 10 minutes and purée in a blender or a food processor. Return the purée to the pot, add the cream, and reheat to the temperature you prefer.

2. Meanwhile, make the croutons: Preheat the oven to 350°F. In a large sauté pan, melt the butter over medium heat. Add the garlic and stir for 1 minute. Add the bread cubes and toss to coat. Spread the cubes on a baking sheet and bake for 15 minutes or until crisp and dry. Check frequently to prevent burning. Let cool.

3. Serve the soup hot with the croutons and garnish with cilantro.

Adrak aur Kari-Patta Rasam

GINGER & CURRY LEAF RASAM

Rasam is an immensely popular South Indian soup. The word *rasam*, in the Tamil language, means "essence," or "juice," and has come to mean a particular type of soup that includes the tartness of tamarind or tomatoes. The ingredients used in *rasam* vary, but it is basically a light, spicy soup. The spiciness can be adjusted to your taste. At times I add vegetables to make this soup a complete meal. | serves 4

- 1/2 cup dried red lentils, picked over, washed, and drained
- 6 1/4 cups water
- 1 teaspoon ground turmeric
- 1/2 teaspoon salt
- 2 tablespoons vegetable oil
- 10 fresh curry leaves
- 2 teaspoons black mustard seeds
- Pinch of ground asafetida
- One 3-inch-long piece fresh ginger, peeled and finely chopped
- 1 medium tomato, finely chopped
- 1 (12-ounce) can unsweetened coconut milk
- 1 tablespoon tamarind paste
- 1 teaspoon freshly ground black pepper

1. Place the lentils, 4 cups water, turmeric, and salt in a large pot and cook over medium-high heat until the lentils are tender, about 30 minutes, frequently skimming off any foam with a spoon.

2. In a heavy-bottom pot, heat the oil over medium heat and add the curry leaves, stirring until very fragrant, about 1 minute. Remove 4 leaves and reserve for the garnish. To the oil, add the mustard seeds, asafetida, ginger, and tomato and cook until the tomato begins to dry, about 3 minutes. Add the lentils with their liquid, 2 1/4 cups water, the coconut milk, tamarind, and black pepper and bring to a boil. Reduce the heat and simmer for another 3 minutes.

3. Season to taste with salt and serve hot, garnished with the fried curry leaves.

Hara Pyaaz aur Mattar Shorba

SPRING ONION & PEA SOUP

- 1 pound fresh or frozen peas, thawed
- 3 spring onions or scallions, chopped
- 3 3/4 cups water or vegetable stock
- 1 teaspoon salt
- 2 tablespoons unsalted butter
- 1/4 cup all-purpose flour
- 1 1/4 cups whole milk
- Freshly ground black pepper

This recipe is a must-try for pea soup lovers. The creamy soup has a nice onion flavor—herb-like, light, and fresh tasting with a pleasant pale green color. I serve it hot with warm, crusty rolls. | serves 4

1. In a medium pot over medium-high heat, bring the peas, onions, water or vegetable stock, and salt to a boil. Reduce the heat and simmer, uncovered, for another 10 minutes. Let cool for 20 minutes and purée the mixture in a blender or food processor. Set aside.

2. Melt the butter in a heavy-bottom pan over medium heat. Stir in the flour and cook for 2 minutes, stirring constantly, to make a roux. Gradually add the milk, stirring constantly, until the roux is dissolved. Bring to a boil, stirring constantly until thickened, about 2 minutes. Stir in the puréed pea mixture and cook until soup is heated through; remove from heat. Season with salt and pepper to taste before serving.

Palak -Jeera Shorba

CUMIN-SCENTED CREAM OF SPINACH SOUP

- 5 tablespoons unsalted butter
- 1 teaspoon cumin seeds
- 1 small white onion, minced
- 5 tablespoons all-purpose flour
- 1 teaspoon salt
- 1/2 teaspoon freshly ground black pepper
- 1/8 teaspoon freshly grated nutmeg
- 4 1/2 cups whole milk
- 1 (10-ounce) package frozen chopped spinach, thawed, and drained well or 1 pound fresh spinach, finely chopped

I love this creamy spinach soup with just a hint of cumin, nutmeg, and black pepper. I've adapted the recipe to make it healthier by substituting milk in place of heavy cream. Using this basic recipe you can prepare creamed soup using your choice of vegetables, such as broccoli or cauliflower. | serves 4

In a medium pot, melt the butter over medium-high heat and add the cumin seeds, stirring until fragrant and darker in color, about 1 minute. Add the onion and sauté until soft, 3 to 4 minutes. Add the flour, salt, pepper, and nutmeg and stir until fragrant, about 3 minutes. Stir in the milk and cook, stirring continuously, until it's bubbly and begins to thicken, about 5 minutes. Stir in the spinach and cook for 2 minutes (if using fresh spinach, allow to cook for a few minutes longer). Serve hot.

Gujrati Kadhi

GUJARATI YOGURT & COCONUT SOUP

- 2 cups plain, lowfat yogurt
- 2 cups water
- 3 tablespoons gram (chickpea) flour
- 2 tablespoons vegetable oil
- 1 teaspoon black mustard seeds
- 4 or 5 fresh curry leaves
- 1 teaspoon ground turmeric
- 1 cup unsweetened coconut milk
- 1/2 teaspoon salt
- 1 ounce broccoli sprouts or other sprouts, for garnish

This soup, from the northwestern region of India, is a favorite of mine and always has me reaching for seconds. Yogurt gives it a tart accent with the added dimension of sweet and mellow coconut milk. The delicious aroma comes from curry leaves, which I add when frying the mustard seeds. | **serves 4**

1. In a blender, combine the yogurt, water, and gram flour and blend until smooth.

2. In a heavy-bottom pot over medium heat, heat the oil, add the mustard seeds, and cook until the seeds start to sputter, about 1 minute. Add the curry leaves and cook, stirring, until very fragrant, about 1 minute. Add the yogurt mixture, turmeric, coconut milk, and salt and bring to a boil. Reduce the heat and simmer for another 5 minutes, stirring constantly, until the mixture is thick and creamy.

3. Garnish with broccoli sprouts and serve hot.

- 4 tablespoons unsalted butter
- 1 medium white onion, chopped
- 2 cloves garlic, finely chopped
- 1 (14 1/2-ounce) can stewed tomatoes, roughly chopped
- 1 (14 1/2-ounce) can chicken broth
- 2 bay leaves
- 2 tablespoons fresh chopped sage
- 1 tablespoon fresh chopped rosemary
- 2 teaspoons fresh chopped thyme
- 1/4 cup water
- 1/3 cup dry white wine, such as Sauvignon blanc
- 1/2 teaspoon salt
- 5 ounces medium shrimp, peeled and deveined
- 5 ounces small bay scallops
- 10 littleneck, manila, or other small clams
- 6 to 7 ounces cod fillets, cut into 1-inch cubes
- Juice of 1 lemon
- 1/2 teaspoon freshly ground black pepper

Machiwala Shorba

FISHERMAN'S SOUP WITH SAGE

In this seafood stew, the blend of sage, rosemary, and thyme creates a wonderfully fragrant broth. The stew also works beautifully as a base that can easily be modified using different varieties of seafood. | serves 4

1. Melt the butter in a large stockpot over medium-low heat. Add the onion and garlic, and cook slowly, stirring occasionally until the onion is soft, about 10 minutes. Add the tomatoes, chicken broth, bay leaves, sage, rosemary, thyme, water, wine, and salt and mix well. Cover and simmer for 30 minutes.

2. Stir in the shrimp, scallops, clams, and cod and bring to a boil. Reduce heat to low, cover, and simmer until clams open, 5 to 7 minutes. Remove the bay leaves and discard.

3. Stir in the lemon juice and adjust the salt and pepper to taste before serving.

580 Blue Sweaters

When I was seventeen, I finally had enough cooking experience to cater a big wedding with the help of two other cooks. It was a great moment in my life. Though it was only for a family wedding, the joy and accomplishment I felt was unlike anything I had experienced before or since. I knew that cooking for others was meant to be my life.

With this momentum, I managed to convince my family to open a catering business. We had rented out the front of our house, but the space was soon to be vacated and perfect for what would become my first business, the Lawrence Gardens Catering Company. As for the most important obstacle, start-up capital, I had big plans.

The local Vivek Public School needed handmade sweaters and its principal, Mrs. Bawa, gave us the job of knitting them. With my mother's help and her amazing ability to take up impossible challenges, we accepted the job. She bought blue wool on credit and we were set to begin making sweaters day and night. But there was just one little problem: Neither of us knew how to knit.

Of course, we went to Biji and she taught us how to knit. Our first attempts were awful. When we took the first samples to the school, Mrs. Bawa looked with regret at the impossibly tiny necklines and reminded us that actual children had to be able to pull the sweaters over their heads to put them on.

It was an important task and I'm still grateful to Mrs. Bawa for having given my family the chance. I remember coming home from school every day and working straight through the night with my Biji and mother, trying to diligently check the quality with sleepy eyes. Though many sweaters were rejected and had to be unraveled and re-knitted, we finally finished 580 blue sweaters just as the days began to shorten and the chilly winds moved in. We made 15,000 rupees, which was about $300 and enough to start the business. It was a very different kind of happiness from what I felt after my first catering job. I'm not sure what exactly I felt that day, but I knew that a dream was about to come true. And so even today, that particular color of blue means hope to me.

Palak aur Akhrot ka Salaad

SPINACH & WALNUT SALAD WITH CURRY DRESSING

The touch of honey in this slightly spicy dressing adds a subtle warmth and comforting taste. Tossed with spinach and toasted walnuts, this salad is easy and satisfying. | **serves 6**

- 2 tablespoons olive oil
- 2 teaspoons cumin seeds
- One 2-inch-long piece fresh ginger, peeled and finely chopped
- 1 teaspoon Madras curry powder (page 23)
- Juice of 1 lemon
- 1 tablespoon honey
- 8 ounces fresh baby spinach, washed and dried
- 10 cherry tomatoes, halved
- 1/2 cup toasted walnuts pieces
- Salt

1. In a small pan, heat the oil over medium heat; add the cumin seeds and cook, stirring, for 1 minute. Add the ginger, curry powder, lemon juice, and honey and cook until fragrant, about 2 minutes. Let cool for 10 minutes.

2. In a large mixing bowl, combine the spinach, tomatoes, and walnuts. Add the curry dressing and gently toss. Season with salt to taste and serve immediately.

Japani Phal ki Chaat

SOYBEAN SPROUT & PERSIMMON SALAD

- 6 ounces soybean sprouts, or bean sprout of your choice
- 1 large ripe Fuyu persimmon, peeled and sliced
- 2 tablespoons golden raisins
- Juice of 2 lemons
- 2 tablespoons finely chopped fresh cilantro
- 1 teaspoon chile flakes
- Salt

Soybean sprouts are garnering increased attention as a vegetable that not only tastes delicious, but is also highly nutritious. In this recipe the sturdy, crunchy sprouts are combined with the Fuyu variety of persimmons, which have exceptional flavor when ripe. | serves 4

Gently toss all the ingredients and season to taste with salt. Serve chilled.

Laal Mooli- Moongfali Chaat

FRENCH BREAKFAST RADISHES WITH MUSTARD SEED DRESSING

- 1 tablespoon olive oil
- 1/4 teaspoon cumin seeds
- 1/4 teaspoon black mustard seeds
- 1 small red onion, minced
- 1/4 teaspoon ground turmeric
- 1/2 teaspoon salt
- 2 cups trimmed and sliced small French breakfast radishes
- 1 tablespoon fresh lemon juice
- 1 cup roasted, chopped peanuts
- 1 tablespoon chopped fresh cilantro

Crisp radishes are the key to this terrific salad. The French breakfast radish has an elongated shape and a red outer skin, which turns white near the roots. This salad was inspired by a breakfast of simply salted radishes I had in France. | serves 4

1. Heat the oil in a small saucepan with a lid over medium heat, add the cumin and mustard seeds, then cover and shake the saucepan until the seeds start to pop, about 2 minutes. Add the onion, turmeric, and salt, cook for 1 minute, then remove from the heat; let cool. This dressing can be kept, covered, in the refrigerator for up to 3 months.

2. Place the radishes in a bowl. Stir the dressing well, and add it to the radishes along with the lemon juice, evenly coating them. Serve topped with peanuts and cilantro.

Nimboowala Kheera Salaad

SUMMER CUCUMBER SALAD WITH LEMON DRESSING

This refreshing, cold cucumber salad is perfect for a summer lunch or dinner. Fresh-squeezed lemons are a must. I also use an array of spices such as turmeric, cumin, sesame, mustard, and nigella seeds. | serves 4

- 1/4 cup plain, lowfat yogurt
- 2 tablespoons sesame seeds, dry-roasted (see page 17) and ground
- 2 teaspoons cumin seeds, dry-roasted (see page 17) and ground
- 1/2 pound cucumbers (about 2 medium cucumbers), peeled, seeded, and diced
- 1/2 pound carrots (about 4 medium carrots), grated
- 1/2 teaspoon salt
- 2 teaspoons mustard oil
- 1/2 teaspoon black mustard seeds
- 1/2 teaspoon nigella seeds
- 1 fresh green chile pepper (such as serrano), slit lengthwise and seeded
- 1/4 teaspoon cayenne pepper
- 1/4 teaspoon ground turmeric
- 1 tablespoon fresh lemon juice
- 2 tablespoons chopped fresh mint leaves

1. In a small bowl, combine the yogurt, sesame seeds, and cumin seeds and mix well to make a smooth paste. Gently mix in the cucumbers, carrots, and salt. Set aside.

2. Heat the mustard oil in a small skillet over medium heat. Add the mustard seeds, nigella seeds, and green chile and cook for about 1 minute, stirring, until the spices are aromatic. Add the cayenne pepper and turmeric. Remove from heat and let cool slightly. Stir the flavored oil and pour it over the cucumber mixture; toss gently. Add the lemon juice and chill for 1 hour before serving. Serve cold, topped with mint leaves.

Phal ki Khatti-Meethi Chaat

TANGY FRUIT SALAD

- 1/2 medium cantaloupe
- 1/2 medium honeydew
- 1/2 small watermelon
- 6 ounces pineapple, cut into 1-inch cubes
- Seeds from 1 pomegranate
- 1 ruby red grapefruit, peeled and cut into 1-inch pieces
- Juice of 1 large or 2 small lemons
- 2 teaspoons mango powder or additional juice of 1 lemon
- 1 tablespoon sugar
- Pinch of salt
- 1 cup finely chopped fresh mint leaves, plus 6 whole leaves for garnish

Dried mango powder is one of my secret ingredients; it brings out the vibrant flavors of the fruits in this dish. This refreshing medley is a wonderful addition to any meal or summer party. | serves 6

1. Using a melon-baller, scoop out balls from the cantaloupe, honeydew, and watermelon. In a large mixing bowl, combine all the ingredients, except the whole mint leaves, until well mixed. Chill in the refrigerator for at least 1 hour before serving.

2. Serve chilled, garnished with whole mint leaves.

3 medium yams (about 1 1/2 pounds), peeled and cut into 1-inch cubes
1/2 teaspoon salt
3 tablespoons sour cream
3 tablespoons tomato paste
1/4 teaspoon freshly ground black pepper
1 cucumber, peeled and diced
1 spring onion or scallion, thinly sliced
1 cup frozen peas, thawed (see Note)
24 pea shoots, for garnish (optional)

Mattar aur Ratalu Chaat

PEA & YAM SALAD

This is a delectable and easy way to cook yams. I find that the sweet-and-spicy tomato dressing mixed with cool cucumber makes the yams and peas perfect partners. | serves 4

1. Place the yams in a pot of salted water; bring to a boil over high heat. Reduce heat to low and simmer, covered, until the yams are just tender, about 30 minutes. Drain and cool to room temperature.

2. In a large mixing bowl, combine the sour cream, tomato paste, salt, and pepper. Add the yams, cucumber, onion, and peas and toss gently until coated with dressing. Garnish with pea shoots, if desired, and serve at room temperature.

note: If fresh peas are available, use them. Simmer 1 cup fresh peas in a quart of lightly salted water for about 3 minutes. Peas from late spring/early summer may take longer to cook, up to 8 minutes.

Vegetables have been the most important ingredient for me since my very early days experimenting in the kitchen with my vegetarian grandmother. In India, vegetarian cuisine is an important part of the culture and has inspired a wealth of meatless dishes.

...

In this chapter, you will find some simple vegetarian dishes as well as some that are a bit more exotic. Feel free to mix and match recipes and techniques with the vegetable of your choice.

PLANTAIN CURRY WITH YOGURT AND CURRY LEAVES

CABBAGE AND MUSHROOMS
IN TURMERIC-INFUSED BUTTER

EGGPLANT WITH SESAME SEEDS AND TAMARIND

GUJARATI-STYLE TINDORA WITH ALMONDS

TURNIPS IN COCONUT AND MUSTARD SEED CURRY

BASIL AND ZUCCHINI WITH YELLOW LENTILS AND GARLIC

DILL, POTATOES, AND RED CHILE

CINNAMON-FLAVORED BUTTERNUT SQUASH
WITH COCONUT

STIR-FRIED PANEER CHEESE WITH MIXED VEGETABLES

SPICE-STUFFED OKRA

STIR-FRIED POTATOES AND GREEN BEANS WITH MINT

BITTER GOURD STUFFED WITH YAMS AND PEANUTS

GINGER-GARLIC PURÉED SPINACH WITH RED POTATOES

Hare kele aur Dahi ki Subzi

PLANTAIN CURRY WITH YOGURT & CURRY LEAVES

Plantains are grown in many parts of India. We treat them as a vegetable when they're green and starchy and as a fruit when they are ripe. In this dish, green plaintains are richly flavored with sautéed curry leaves, mustard seeds, and split peas. I simmer the mixture in yogurt and coconut milk to yield a rich, smooth result, flavored with tamarind and red chiles. | **serves 4**

- 3 green plantains, peeled and cut into 1/2-inch rounds
- 2 tablespoons tamarind paste
- 1 teaspoon ground turmeric
- 1/2 teaspoon salt
- 1 1/4 cups water
- 3 tablespoons vegetable oil
- 8 to 10 fresh curry leaves
- 1 tablespoon black mustard seeds
- 1 teaspoon dried split peas
- 1 dried hot red chile pepper, halved lengthwise
- Pinch of ground asafetida
- 1 tablespoon curry powder (page 23)
- 1 cup unsweetened coconut milk
- 1/2 cup plain, lowfat yogurt, whisked smooth

1. Place the plantains, tamarind paste, turmeric, salt, and water in a medium pot with a lid over high heat and bring to a boil. Reduce the heat to low, cover, and simmer until the plantains are tender and cooked through, 10 to 12 minutes.

2. In a medium skillet, heat the oil over medium heat and fry the curry leaves until very fragrant, about 2 minutes. Remove leaves and reserve.

3. Add the mustard seeds and split peas to the infused oil and fry until crackling, about 2 minutes. Add the dried chile, asafetida, curry powder, and the plantains with their cooking liquid and cook, stirring until well combined. Add the coconut milk and stir. Reduce the heat to low and gently add the yogurt a little at a time to avoid curdling. Stir until the sauce is thick and smooth in texture.

4. Season to taste with salt and serve warm, garnished with the fried curry leaves.

Khumbh aur Bandh Gobi

CABBAGE & MUSHROOMS IN TURMERIC-INFUSED BUTTER

- 2 tablespoons unsalted butter
- 1 teaspoon black mustard seeds
- 1 teaspoon cumin seeds
- 2 cloves garlic, minced
- One 1-inch-long piece fresh ginger, peeled and minced
- 1 tablespoon ground turmeric
- 1 small green cabbage (about 1 1/2 pounds), cored and shredded
- 1 cup thinly sliced button mushrooms
- 1 teaspoon garam masala (page 25)
- 1 teaspoon cayenne pepper
- 1/2 teaspoon salt
- Juice of 1 lemon

This is a simple, quick, and flexible recipe. The cabbage and mushrooms resonate with the slight pungency of the turmeric and the spicy, nutty flavors of the other spices. I sometimes use green peas instead of mushrooms when making this dish. You can, of course, substitute any other type of mushroom. | serves 4 to 6

1. Heat the butter in a medium wok or skillet with a lid over medium heat. Add the mustard seeds and fry until crackling, about 2 minutes. Add the cumin seeds and cook until darker in color and fragrant, about 1 minute. Add the garlic, ginger, and turmeric and cook until the garlic begins to brown, about 2 minutes. Add the cabbage, mushrooms, garam masala, cayenne pepper, and salt and stir until all the ingredients are well combined. Reduce the heat to low, cover, and cook until the cabbage is tender, about 15 minutes, adding a few tablespoons of water if necessary.

2. Stir in the lemon juice, adjust the salt to taste, and serve hot.

3 tablespoons vegetable oil

1 1/2 pounds eggplant (about 2 medium eggplants), stemmed and cut into 1-inch cubes

1 teaspoon salt

1/4 teaspoon freshly ground black pepper

2 dried hot red chile peppers, crushed

6 tablespoons sesame seeds

2 medium red onions, finely chopped

1/2 teaspoon ground turmeric

2 cloves garlic, minced

3 tablespoons tamarind paste

1 cup water

2 tablespoons finely chopped fresh cilantro, for garnish

Khatte- Meethe Baingan

EGGPLANT WITH SESAME SEEDS & TAMARIND

A variation of a classic Indian eggplant dish, this recipe showcases the flavor of eggplant when combined with sesame seeds, turmeric, and tamarind paste. | serves 4 to 6

1. Heat 2 tablespoons oil in a large skillet over medium heat. Add the eggplant, salt, and pepper and stir-fry until the skin turns light brown, 8 to 10 minutes. Remove from the skillet.

2. Add the remaining tablespoon of oil to the skillet over medium heat. Add the dried chiles, sesame seeds, onions, turmeric, and garlic and cook until the onions begin to brown, 4 to 5 minutes. Add the stir-fried eggplants and tamarind paste and stir until the eggplant is evenly coated. Add the water and cook, stirring, until semidry and the eggplant is tender and cooked through, about 10 minutes. Add a little more water if needed.

3. Season with salt and pepper to taste and serve garnished with cilantro.

Tindora-Badam Masala

GUJARATI-STYLE TINDORA WITH ALMONDS

Tindora, or ivy gourd, comes from the cucumber family. It can be found in Indian grocery stores in the vegetable section. A friend of mine has made this successfully with Kirby cucumbers in place of the *tindora*; the cooking time is about five minutes longer. This recipe follows the Gujarati style of cuisine from the northwest region of India, which is predominantly vegetarian and slightly sweet. It is common to add a little sugar or *jaggery*, (a type of unrefined sugar ground in a mortar and pestle) to most Gujarati recipes. If *tindora* is not in season, I use the frozen kind, which works equally well in the recipe. | serves 4

- 2 tablespoons vegetable oil
- 1 teaspoon black mustard seeds
- 1 tablespoon finely chopped garlic
- 1 fresh green chile pepper (such as serrano), seeded and minced
- 1 teaspoon ground cumin
- 1 tablespoon ground coriander
- 16 ounces fresh *tindora*, washed, dried, and halved lengthwise
- 1/2 cup water
- 1/2 teaspoon ground turmeric
- 1 teaspoon salt
- 2 tablespoons light brown sugar
- Juice of 1/2 lemon
- 2 tablespoons unsweetened coconut flakes (optional)
- 2 tablespoons toasted almond slivers (optional)

1. Heat the oil in a heavy-bottom skillet with a lid over medium heat. Add the mustard seeds and cook until crackling, about 2 minutes. Add the garlic and green chile and cook until softened, 2 to 3 minutes. Stir in the cumin, coriander, and *tindora* and cook, about 2 minutes. Add the water, turmeric, salt, brown sugar, and lemon juice and mix well. Reduce the heat to low and simmer, covered, until the *tindora* are tender and cooked, 12 to 15 minutes. Adjust the salt to taste.

2. Garnish with the coconut flakes and almonds before serving, if desired.

Nariyal wale Shalgam

TURNIPS IN COCONUT & MUSTARD SEED CURRY

- 1/4 cup vegetable oil
- 1 tablespoon black mustard seeds
- 1 tablespoon finely chopped garlic
- 1 small red onion, finely chopped
- 1 fresh green chile pepper (such as serrano), seeded and minced
- 1 teaspoon ground cumin
- 1 tablespoon ground coriander
- 1 medium tomato, peeled, seeded, and finely chopped
- 1 pound tender turnips, peeled and cut into 1-inch pieces
- 1 cup unsweetened coconut milk
- 1/2 teaspoon ground turmeric
- 1 teaspoon salt
- 1 cup water
- 1/4 cup chopped fresh dill, for garnish

This dish, a family favorite since childhood, is best enjoyed on sunny winter afternoons when sweet, juicy turnips are in season. The mustard seeds add a fresh aroma and pungent flavor. Cooking the turnips in coconut milk adds a South Indian touch. | serves 4

1. Heat the oil in a heavy-bottom skillet over medium heat. Add the mustard seeds and cook until crackling, about 2 minutes. Add the garlic, onion, and green chile and cook until onion turns golden brown, 4 to 5 minutes. Stir in the cumin, coriander, and tomato and cook, 5 to 7 minutes. Add the turnips, coconut milk, turmeric, and salt and mix until all the ingredients are well combined. Add the water and cook, stirring occasionally, until the turnips are cooked, 15 to 20 minutes. Increase the heat to high and cook until any remaining water is evaporated, about 3 minutes.

2. Serve hot, garnished with dill.

Peeli Daal aur Tori

BASIL & ZUCCHINI WITH YELLOW LENTILS & GARLIC

- 1 cup dried yellow lentils, picked over, rinsed, and drained
- 1/2 teaspoon ground turmeric
- 1 teaspoon salt
- 4 cups water
- 2 tablespoons vegetable oil
- 6 cloves garlic, crushed
- 1 teaspoon cumin seeds
- 1 small white onion, thinly sliced
- 4 small zucchini, cut into 1/2-inch slices
- 1 tablespoon ground coriander
- 1 teaspoon ground cumin
- 1/2 teaspoon paprika
- 1/2 cup coarsely chopped fresh basil leaves
- 2 tablespoons chopped fresh cilantro

Fresh zucchini, basil, garlic, and yellow lentils are cooked together with paprika, cumin, and coriander. Traditionally, basil is not used in Indian cooking, but the addition here gives the dish a fresh taste. | serves 6

1. Put the lentils into a large saucepan with a lid, along with the turmeric, salt, and water. Bring to a boil over high heat, skimming off any froth that may rise to the top. Reduce the heat to low and simmer, covered, until the lentils are cooked, 15 to 20 minutes. Adjust the salt to taste and transfer lentils with cooking liquid to a serving bowl. Cover the bowl and keep warm.

2. Heat the oil in a medium saucepan over medium heat. Add the garlic and cook until golden brown, about 5 minutes. Add the cumin seeds; they should sizzle on contact with the hot oil. Quickly add the onion, zucchini, coriander, and cumin and cook over medium heat until the zucchini becomes tender but not mushy, about 10 minutes. Remove the pan from the heat, add the paprika and basil, and immediately pour the mixture over the hot lentils, stirring lightly to mix. Sprinkle the cilantro on top and serve hot.

Lawrence Gardens Catering Company

My grandfather grew up in Punjab with no border between India and Pakistan. Lahore, the cultural capital of this area, was his favorite city and he always missed Lawrence Gardens, the main public garden there. His love of the city came out like poetry and the get-togethers there with family and friends were still vivid in his memory. Though I could not bring any of his cherished moments back, I named my first catering company Lawrence Gardens.

On December 2, 1990 we officially opened Lawrence Gardens, inaugurated by Biji, my mother, and Mrs. Bawa. It was a small space in the beginning, but it was ours. My pride was much greater than the facility. For the sign, I obtained a huge board and hand-painted it bold shades of green and red. I still remember carrying the sign two miles to save the cost of a rickshaw.

Cooking for passion and running a business turned out to be two entirely different things. Through favorable word of mouth and my mother's circle of acquaintances, we had some business going, but for the first six months made no more than 10,000 rupees in sales, which was about $200. We couldn't afford our own staff and equipment, so for each party we booked, we went to the vegetable market (*mandi*), hired people, and rented tables, cookware, plateware—everything on the spot. Since we didn't even have refrigerators and there is no thought of wasting food in India, the staff took home all the food after each completed job. Yet through all of our initial struggles, the thought that scared me most was: Where would I cook if we ever had to close this?

My prayers were soon answered when we landed regular catering jobs from the local bank and school. We were able to buy our own equipment and slowly but steadily, Biji's food became famous. When it comes to their food, Indian people consider themselves to be fully qualified food critics—the criticism was relentless as guests compared the food to their own mother and grandmother's dishes. I knew I was blessed to have had my Biji as a teacher. We soon began booking even more clients and our reputation became better established. Finally, the Lawrence Gardens Catering Company was really in business.

Aloo-Savaa Bhaji

DILL, POTATOES & RED CHILE

In this dish, the deep flavor of the russet potatoes is nicely offset by intensely fragrant dill. I always add fresh dill at the end of the cooking time, as it loses its flavor when heated too long. | serves 4

- 1 pound russet potatoes (about 3 potatoes), peeled and diced
- 1/4 cup vegetable oil
- 5 cloves garlic, minced
- 2 teaspoons black mustard seeds
- 2 dried red chile peppers
- 1 tablespoon Madras curry powder (page 23)
- 1/2 cup chopped fresh dill
- Salt

1. Place potatoes in a large pot of cold water and bring to a boil. Reduce heat to low and simmer, covered, until fork-tender, 15 to 20 minutes. Drain and set potatoes aside.

2. Heat the oil in a heavy-bottom saucepan with a lid over medium-high heat. Add the garlic and fry for 30 seconds. Add the mustard seeds and dried chiles, cover, and briefly allow the seeds to pop. Stir in the potatoes and curry powder and sauté until well combined and fragrant, 3 to 4 minutes. Add the dill, cover, and cook over low heat for 2 minutes. Season with salt to taste and serve hot.

Daalchini aur Nariyal wala Kaddu

CINNAMON-FLAVORED BUTTERNUT SQUASH WITH COCONUT

- 2 tablespoons vegetable oil
- 1/2 teaspoon cumin seeds
- 2 dried red chile peppers, stemmed
- One 1-inch-long piece cinnamon stick
- 2 bay leaves
- 1 cup chopped red onion
- 1 1/2 pounds butternut squash (1 large squash), peeled and diced
- 1 teaspoon ground coriander
- 1 tablespoon light brown sugar
- 1/2 teaspoon salt
- 1/2 cup dried, grated unsweetened coconut flakes
- 1/2 cup water
- 1/4 cup chopped fresh cilantro

I find butternut to be more flavorful than other varieties of both summer and winter squash. In this wintery dish, it is flavored with cinnamon and other spices and garnished with fresh cilantro. Cinnamon and cumin work well with butternut squash, adding both a savory and sweet flavor. | serves 4

1. Heat the oil in a large, heavy skillet over medium-high heat. Add the cumin seeds, dried chiles, cinnamon stick, and bay leaves and fry briefly, 1 minute. Add the onion and cook, stirring frequently, until golden brown, about 5 minutes. Add the squash; lower the heat to medium and cook, stirring constantly to prevent sticking, 5 minutes. Add the coriander, brown sugar, and salt and cook for another 2 minutes, until the squash has softened. Add the coconut and stir to break up lumps and blend it into the squash. Add the water. Cook for 2 to 3 minutes, stirring occasionally to prevent sticking. Taste for seasonings, and adjust if necessary. Discard the bay leaves.

2. Garnish with chopped cilantro before serving.

- 3 tablespoons vegetable oil
- 1 tablespoon peeled, minced fresh ginger
- 2 large cloves garlic, minced
- 2 small red onions, diced
- 2 tablespoons ground coriander
- 1 teaspoon ground cumin
- 1/2 teaspoon ground fennel
- 1/2 teaspoon ground cardamom
- 1/2 teaspoon red pepper flakes
- 1/2 teaspoon salt
- 4 small tomatoes, diced
- 2 small green bell peppers, diced
- 2 small red bell peppers, diced
- 2 small yellow bell peppers, diced
- 6 ounces paneer cheese, diced
- 1/4 cup chopped fresh cilantro
- 4 scallions, trimmed, white part cut diagonally into 1/4-inch slices
- Freshly ground black pepper

Kadhai Paneer

STIR-FRIED PANEER CHEESE WITH MIXED VEGETABLES

This healthy and easy recipe features mixed vegetables, paneer, and a blend of spices. Stir-frying briefly, on high heat, helps the different elements retain their texture and bright flavor. | serves 6

1. Heat the oil in a large, nonstick wok or skillet over medium-high heat. Add the ginger and garlic and cook, stirring, about 1 minute. Add the onions and continue cooking, stirring, until golden, 2 to 3 minutes. Add the coriander, cumin, fennel, cardamom, pepper flakes, and salt. Stir-fry over medium heat, about 2 minutes. Add the tomatoes and bell peppers, and continue to cook, stirring constantly, until the dish is saucy, about 5 minutes.

2. Add the paneer, cilantro, and scallions and cook over medium-high heat, uncovered, about 5 minutes. Serve hot, sprinkled with black pepper.

Bhindi Masala

SPICE-STUFFED OKRA

1 tablespoon ground coriander
1 teaspoon ground cumin
1 teaspoon mango powder
1 teaspoon ground fennel
1/2 teaspoon ground turmeric
1/2 teaspoon garam masala (page 25)
1/4 teaspoon paprika
1/4 teaspoon cayenne pepper
1 teaspoon salt
1 1/2 pounds fresh tender okra, rinsed and patted dry
3 tablespoons vegetable oil
1 1/2 teaspoons cumin seeds
1 large red onion, cut in half lengthwise and thinly sliced
2 tablespoons chopped fresh cilantro, for garnish

This recipe is a family favorite. I slit the okra lengthwise, fill it with a medley of spices, and cook it until golden brown and crisp. | serves 6

1. In a small bowl, mix together the first 8 spices and the salt.

2. Cut off the very end of each okra stem and discard. Then make a long slit on one side from the stem down, stopping 3/4 inch from the tip. (This forms a pocket for the stuffing but keeps the okra intact.) Stuff 1/4 to 1/2 teaspoon of the spice mixture into each okra pocket and reserve any leftover spice mixture.

3. Heat 2 tablespoons oil in a flat, heavy-bottom nonstick skillet over medium-high heat. Add the cumin seeds; they should sizzle upon contact with the hot oil. Quickly add the onion and cook, stirring, over medium-high heat until golden, about 5 minutes. With a slotted spoon, transfer mixture to a bowl.

4. In same skillet, lay all the stuffed okra in a single layer. Drizzle the remaining 1 tablespoon of oil on top and cook over medium-low heat, turning the pieces very carefully, until tender, 15 to 20 minutes.

5. Scatter the cooked onion over the okra and then add any leftover spice mixture. Mix carefully and cook over medium-low heat, turning occasionally, until brown and crisp, about 5 minutes. Transfer to a serving dish and serve garnished with fresh chopped cilantro.

Kadhai Subzi

STIR-FRIED POTATOES & GREEN BEANS WITH MINT

A Chinese exchange student who lived with me one summer in Mumbai taught me this delicious recipe. Crisp, bright green beans are first blanched until tender and then tossed together in a wok with potatoes and spices. Make sure the oil is very hot so the vegetables get the grilled, smoky flavor typical of stir-fries. | serves 6

- 8 medium Yukon gold potatoes, washed
- 1/2 pound fresh green beans, trimmed
- 3 tablespoons vegetable oil
- 1 tablespoon black mustard seeds
- 1 tablespoon cumin seeds
- 1 teaspoon ground turmeric
- 2 medium tomatoes, coarsely chopped
- 1 teaspoon salt
- 2 fresh green chile peppers (such as serrano), seeded and minced
- 4 scallions, chopped
- 1/4 cup chopped fresh mint leaves
- Juice of 1 lemon

1. Place the potatoes in a large pot with cold water to cover; bring to a boil over high heat. Reduce heat to low and simmer, uncovered, until just cooked through but still firm, 25 to 30 minutes. (Test the largest potato in the pot by piercing it with a fork; it should be firm but cooked at the center.) Drain and set aside to cool.

2. Meanwhile, bring another pot of water to a boil. Add the green beans and cook until just tender, 2 to 3 minutes. Drain, rinse under cold water, and drain again.

3. Cut the beans into 1- to 1 1/2-inch-long pieces and set aside. Peel the potatoes and cut them into 1-inch cubes. Set them aside.

4. Heat the oil in a wok or a wide, heavy pot over medium-high heat. Add the mustard seeds. When they have popped for 30 seconds, add the cumin seeds and turmeric, stir briefly, and then stir in the tomatoes and salt. Stir-fry for about 1 minute. Add the potatoes and stir-fry for another minute. Stir in the green chiles, scallions, green beans, mint, and lemon juice. Remove from the heat; taste for salt and adjust if necessary. Serve hot.

Bharwa Karela

BITTER GOURD STUFFED WITH YAMS & PEANUTS

- 1 large yam, peeled and diced
- 1/2 cup chopped dry-roasted peanuts (see page 17)
- 2 tablespoons salt
- 1 teaspoon ground cumin
- 1 tablespoon ground coriander
- 1 teaspoon cayenne pepper
- 1 teaspoon *chaat masala* (page 20) (optional)
- 2 tablespoons finely chopped fresh mint leaves
- 8 tender medium-size bitter gourds
- 8 cups water
- 16 scallions
- 3 tablespoons vegetable oil
- 1 tablespoon cumin seeds
- 2 tablespoons finely chopped garlic

Bitter gourd is a popular vegetable in Indian cooking. It does have a bitter taste, which can be reduced by rubbing salt on it and boiling it. Garlic or chile peppers also help to offset the bitter taste. The preferred preparation is to stuff the gourd with potatoes or ground spices. Here I have used a spiced mixture of yams and peanuts as the filling. | serves 4 to 6

1. Place the diced yam in a large pot with cold water, cover, and bring to a boil. Reduce heat to low and simmer until just cooked through but still firm (test the largest piece of yam by piercing it with a fork; it should be firm but cooked at the center), 15 minutes. Drain and let cool to room temperature. Mash the yams with a wire masher.

2. Combine the mashed yams with the peanuts, salt to taste, cumin, coriander, cayenne pepper, *chaat masala* (if desired), and mint in a medium, nonreactive (stainless steel or glass) mixing bowl and mix well.

3. Lightly scrape the bumpy outer surface from each gourd with a vegetable peeler and gently make a slit on one side so you can reach inside with a finger to remove all the seeds.

4. Add 2 tablespoons salt to 8 cups of water in a deep pot and place over high heat. When the water comes to a boil, add the gourds and blanch until soft, about 4 minutes. Remove the gourds with a slotted spoon but leave the water boiling. Let gourds cool to room temperature. Squeeze out excess water; this helps reduce the bitterness of the gourds.

5. Trim off the white ends of the scallions and blanch the green tops in the same boiling water, 30 seconds. Refresh under cold running water and set aside on a paper towel.

6. Stuff the gourds with the yam mixture through the slit. Gently tie 2 blanched scallions around the bitter gourd to secure the stuffing.

7. Pour the oil into a heavy-bottom saucepan or skillet large enough to hold all the stuffed gourds in one layer and place over medium-low heat. Add the stuffed gourds and cook, covered, for 5 to 7 minutes, until the gourds turn golden brown. Gently flip the gourds over and continue cooking until they are nicely browned and cooked through, another 10 to 12 minutes. Drain gourds on a kitchen towel to remove excess oil.

8. Heat the same skillet over high heat and add the cumin seeds and garlic and cook until the garlic is lightly browned and the cumin seeds are toasted, 2 to 3 minutes. Pour this over the gourds on a serving plate. Serve hot.

Aloo Palak

GINGER-GARLIC PURÉED SPINACH WITH RED POTATOES

Spinach can be substituted with any other greens such as collards or beet greens. I simmer the puréed spinach for fifteen to twenty minutes at the end, until the spinach becomes velvety smooth. | serves 4

- Two 1-inch-long pieces fresh ginger, peeled
- 2 cloves garlic
- 2 fresh green chile peppers (such as serrano)
- 1 pound fresh or frozen, thawed, spinach, chopped
- 1 cup water
- 2 tablespoons vegetable oil
- 1 teaspoon cumin seeds
- 1 medium red onion, finely chopped
- 1 pound red potatoes, skin on, diced
- 1 tablespoon ground coriander
- 1 teaspoon garam masala (page 25)
- 1/2 teaspoon paprika
- 1 teaspoon salt
- 2 medium tomatoes, chopped
- Lemon wedges, for serving

1. In a food processor or a blender, add the ginger, garlic, and green chiles; blend until minced. Add the spinach and water, process again to make a coarse purée.

2. Heat the oil in a large, nonstick saucepan with a lid over medium-high heat and add the cumin seeds. Quickly add the onion and sauté, stirring, until golden, 2 to 3 minutes. Add the potatoes and cook, stirring, for about 3 minutes. Mix in the coriander, garam masala, paprika, and salt.

3. Add the tomatoes and cook, stirring, for about 5 minutes. Mix in the puréed spinach and cook, stirring, until it comes to a boil. Reduce the heat to low and simmer, covered, until the potatoes are cooked, 15 to 20 minutes. Stir up the potatoes from the bottom every 5 minutes. If the sauce seems a little thin, leave the cover off for the last 5 minutes to reduce. Adjust salt to taste.

4. Serve hot with lemon wedges.

POULTRY

Chicken still reminds me of Sunday lunches. Growing up, it was the only day of the week when we had chicken at home. I used to go to the market with my grandfather to pick up the chicken, and my grandmother, who was a vegetarian, would have me come into the kitchen to taste test the dish to make sure it was ready.

. . .

Chicken is ideal for curries and sauces because its mild flavor does not overpower the seasonings. This section features home-style curries as well as more involved dishes that are perfect for entertaining. Home-style curries are generally more roughly textured than restaurant curries, allowing you to taste the many flavors of the ingredients.

Murg Masala Shahad Wala

MASALA-HONEY CORNISH HENS

Four 1-pound Cornish hens, room temperature, rinsed well and patted dry

1/2 teaspoon salt

1/4 cup honey

2 tablespoons soy sauce

Juice of 2 lemons

1/4 cup garam masala (page 25)

1/4 cup lavender flowers, ground, plus 8 sprigs for garnish

1/4 cup olive oil

Everyone appreciates lavender for its scent and pretty flowers, but very few people have tasted it. Lavender brings an unusual herbal, slightly floral flavor to the Cornish hens. I recommend grinding the lavender with a mortar and pestle or food processor. | serves 4

1. Preheat the oven to 400°F. Season the hens with salt and set aside for 10 minutes. In a medium mixing bowl, combine the honey, soy sauce, lemon juice, garam masala, and lavender flowers. Evenly rub the hens with the marinade and let them rest for another 10 minutes.

2. In a large, heavy-bottom skillet, heat the oil over medium-high heat. Sear the hens on all sides. Transfer hens to a roasting pan; roast in the oven until the hens are tender and cooked, and a thermometer inserted into the thigh reads 165°F, about 30 minutes. Arrange on a platter and serve garnished with lavender sprigs.

- 2 tablespoons olive oil
- 2 pounds boneless skinless chicken breasts, cut into 1-inch pieces
- 6 green cardamom pods
- One 1-inch-long piece cinnamon stick
- 2 medium white onions, finely chopped
- 2 cloves garlic, finely chopped
- One 2-inch-long piece fresh ginger, peeled and finely chopped
- 1 cup coarsely chopped fresh dill
- 2 tomatoes, finely chopped
- 2 teaspoons ground turmeric
- 1 teaspoon ground cumin
- 1 teaspoon cayenne pepper
- 1 cup water
- 1 teaspoon salt
- Basmati rice (page 78), for serving

Elaichiwala Murg

DILL & CARDAMOM CHICKEN

The strong and aromatic flavor of cardamom is a great complement to the flavor of dill. Cinnamon, garlic, and ginger enhance the flavor of the oil in which the chicken is cooked. The resulting taste is a refreshing blend of distinctive flavors. | serves 4 to 6

1. Heat the oil in a large saucepan over medium-high heat. Stir-fry the chicken in batches until lightly golden, about 2 minutes. Remove with a slotted spoon.

2. To the same saucepan, add the cardamom, cinnamon, onions, garlic, and ginger. Stir-fry until spices become aromatic, 1 to 2 minutes. Add the reserved chicken, dill, tomatoes, turmeric, cumin, cayenne pepper, and water. Slowly bring to a boil, stirring occasionally. Reduce heat to low and simmer, uncovered, until the chicken pieces are cooked, about 30 minutes. Add a little water if necessary. Adjust the seasoning with salt and serve hot with basmati rice.

Murg Tikka Masala

CHICKEN TIKKA MASALA

Although the origins of this famous dish are unclear, one thing is certain: it's delicious. Popularly referred to as the national dish of the U.K., Chicken Tikka Masala is also a favorite of millions around the U.S. The tender pieces of chicken are simmered in a sauce of tomatoes and cream with fenugreek leaves. | serves 4 to 6

FOR THE CHICKEN:

- One 2-to-3-inch-long piece fresh ginger, peeled and coarsely chopped
- 4 cloves garlic
- 1/2 teaspoon salt
- 1/2 teaspoon cayenne pepper
- 1/2 teaspoon garam masala (page 25)
- Juice of 1 lemon
- 1/4 cup plain, lowfat yogurt, plus more for garnish
- 2 tablespoons vegetable oil
- 2 pounds boneless, skinless chicken breast, cut into 1-inch pieces

FOR THE SAUCE:

- 2 tablespoons butter or ghee
- 1 medium red onion, chopped
- 1 fresh green chile pepper (such as serrano), chopped
- 2 cloves garlic, minced
- 3 green cardamom pods, lightly crushed
- 2 teaspoons ground cumin
- 2 tablespoons curry powder (page 23)
- 2 tablespoons paprika
- 2 tablespoons dried fenugreek leaves
- 3 tablespoons tomato paste
- 1/4 cup water
- 1 cup tomato purée
- 1 cup heavy cream
- Sweetened coconut flakes, for garnish (optional)
- Salt
- Basmati rice (page 78), for serving

1. To prepare the chicken, combine the ginger, garlic, salt, cayenne pepper, garam masala, and lemon juice in a blender. Starting on medium speed, pulse the machine and scrape down the sides as necessary. Gradually increase the speed until you have a fairly smooth paste. In a large bowl, combine the paste with the yogurt and oil. Add the chicken and mix until the chicken is evenly coated. Cover the bowl and marinate in the refrigerator for 4 hours or overnight.

2. To make the sauce, melt the butter or ghee in a large, heavy skillet over medium heat. Sauté the onion until well cooked, 10 to 15 minutes. Add the green chile and garlic and cook until well caramelized, about 10 minutes. Add the cardamom, cumin, curry powder, paprika, and fenugreek leaves, and cook, stirring well, until the mixture is fragrant, about 2 minutes. Stir in the tomato paste and cook for 5 minutes, stirring frequently. Deglaze the pan with the water then stir in the tomato purée. Bring to a boil over high heat, then remove the sauce from the heat. Let cool slightly.

3. Remove the chicken from the refrigerator about 20 minutes before you plan on serving it. Heat a grill or grill pan over medium-high heat and grill the chicken until it is fully cooked and tender, about 10 minutes. This can be done in the broiler as well, also for about 10 minutes.

4. Purée the sauce in a blender until smooth. Return the sauce to the skillet over medium heat and add the cream, stirring well; add the chicken. Simmer over low heat until the sauce thickens, about 10 minutes. Season with salt to taste, transfer to a serving dish, and garnish with coconut flakes and yogurt on the side. Serve with basmati rice.

Bharwa Murg Khumb ke Saath

MUSHROOM-STUFFED ROAST CHICKEN

This variation on traditional tandoori chicken uses a wonderfully savory filling of mushrooms and white wine. The mushrooms add a new flavor to this classic dish and make for an exceptionally juicy chicken. | serves 4

1 (3-pound) whole chicken, rinsed and dried

1/2 teaspoon salt

1/2 teaspoon freshly ground black pepper

3 tablespoons olive oil

1/2 medium red onion, finely chopped

1 tablespoon finely chopped garlic

8 ounces cremini mushrooms, finely chopped

1 teaspoon garam masala (page 25)

1/2 cup white wine, such as Riesling or Gewürztraminer

1/3 cup ghee or vegetable oil

1. Preheat the oven to 375°F. Generously season the chicken with salt and pepper and set aside for 10 minutes.

2. In a medium skillet, heat the olive oil over medium heat and cook the onion and garlic until softened, about 5 minutes; add the mushrooms and garam masala and cook until the mushrooms begin to release their juices, about 5 minutes. Add the wine and continue to cook until all the liquid is evaporated, about 5 minutes. Set aside and let cool.

3. Using your fingers or the back of a spoon, loosen the skin from chicken breast. Stuff the mushroom mixture under the skin, pressing it into an even 1/2-inch layer. Tie the legs of the bird together with kitchen twine. Brush the chicken generously with ghee or oil.

4. In a large, heavy-bottom, ovenproof skillet heat the remaining ghee or oil, add the chicken, breast side down, and cook over medium-high heat until browned, about 4 minutes. Turn the chicken over. Transfer the skillet to the oven and roast the chicken for 40 to 45 minutes or until a thermometer inserted into the thickest part of the thigh reads 165°F. To further test for doneness, pierce the thigh. If the juices run clear, the chicken is cooked through.

5. Arrange chicken on a platter and let rest for 15 minutes before serving.

Punjabi Murg Curry

NORTH INDIAN–STYLE CHICKEN CURRY

Tender pieces of chicken breast are simmered in chicken stock with tomatoes and spices in this old family recipe, which, to me, is comfort food. Curry should be cooked slowly for a long time to get the best flavor. The degree of spiciness can be adjusted to suit your taste. The result tastes great over rice or with naan. | serves 4 to 6

- 4 boneless, skinless chicken breasts (about 2 pounds), cut into 1-inch pieces
- Salt and freshly ground black pepper
- 1/4 cup ghee or vegetable oil
- 3 medium onions, finely chopped
- 4 medium tomatoes, finely chopped
- 1 tablespoon tomato paste
- 3 tablespoons minced garlic
- 3 tablespoons peeled, minced fresh ginger
- 2 fresh green chile peppers (such as serrano), seeded and chopped
- 1 teaspoon cumin seeds
- 1 teaspoon ground turmeric
- 1 bay leaf
- 2 tablespoons garam masala (page 25)
- 2 cups chicken stock
- Naan (102) or basmati rice (page 78), for serving

1. Season the chicken with salt and pepper and set aside. Heat the ghee or oil in a large saucepan with a lid over medium heat and sauté the onions until soft and transparent, about 5 minutes. Add the tomatoes, tomato paste, garlic, ginger, green chiles, cumin seeds, turmeric, bay leaf, and garam masala. Cook, covered, until the tomatoes are well softened, about 5 minutes.

2. Add the chicken and chicken stock. Bring to a boil, stirring occasionally. Reduce the heat to low and simmer, uncovered, until chicken is tender, about 30 minutes. If the sauce seems too thin you can bring it up to a boil for 5 minutes or so to reduce. Adjust the seasoning with salt and pepper to taste. Remove the bay leaf and serve hot with fresh naan or basmati rice, if desired.

A Culinary Education

In 1991, my uncle, Baboo Chacha, invited me to visit him in Delhi. I had visited Delhi a few times before for summer vacations, but had seen little of the city. This time it was different—we would be going to the Maurya Sheraton Hotel for a special midnight buffet. There I saw for the first time the art associated with food: the aesthetics, the variety, and the care given to the presentation of the cakes and pastries. The whole thing exploded in my mind—it was as though the earth had shifted and I was given new eyes. It was so far from my world of experience that I was profoundly shocked. My heart was hammering in my chest as I realized that food was also art and could rise to astonishing levels of beauty. I stuttered and babbled. I could barely carry my plate. I was so nervous that I felt sick, unable to eat though my plate was packed with beautiful delicacies. I was filled with a sense of wonder that has inspired me to become the chef I am today. I have never forgotten that experience.

It was Baboo Chacha who advised me to study the culinary arts and seek admission to the Welcomgroup Graduate School of Hotel Administration in Manipal. When I decided that food was going to be my life and that there was no better place to learn than Welcomgroup, the decision came easily: I dropped everything to make this dream come true. After leaving the catering business to my mother and Biji, I enrolled in the school and my future unfolded from there.

Everything I knew about food up to that point went out the window. For the next three years while I worked and studied, I saw things that only made me want to see more of the world. I travelled throughout India—first south to Madras then north to Kashmir, to Nepal, and finally to Mumbai, the culinary capital of India.

I was intimidated at first by the grand scope and history of Indian cuisine. It was far more diverse than I ever knew from my experiences growing up. Every region has its own distinctive cuisine and there was so much to learn. Every day my mind was opened to new foods that I had never tried before, never even imagining that these different foods existed. It went well beyond my imagination. When I finished my culinary education at the WelcomGroup, I was a different person.

Bhattiwala Murg

THE RUBIN MUSEUM'S CURRY-CRUSTED CHICKEN

When I collaborate with the Rubin Museum in New York City for events, we often reinvent classic Indian dishes to suit a more contemporary palate. Our take on chicken *tikka* uses whole chicken breasts instead of the traditional diced chicken. It is a terrific dish for summer barbecuing. | serves 6

- 1 teaspoon ground cumin
- 1 teaspoon ground coriander
- 2 cups sour cream
- 4 cloves garlic, chopped
- 2 tablespoons peeled, chopped fresh ginger
- 3 tablespoons vegetable oil
- 2 tablespoons fresh lemon juice
- 1 teaspoon grated lemon zest
- 1 teaspoon salt
- 1/2 teaspoon freshly ground black pepper
- 1/2 teaspoon ground turmeric
- 3 tablespoons Madras curry powder (page 23)
- 1 teaspoon cayenne pepper
- 6 (8-ounce) boneless, skinless chicken breasts
- 6 lemon wedges, for garnish

1. Mix all ingredients except chicken and lemon wedges in a large bowl. If you prefer a perfectly smooth texture you can process this mixture in a blender.

2. Place the chicken in the bowl, fully coating each piece with the sour cream mixture. Cover tightly and refrigerate for 4 to 6 hours. Remove the chicken from the refrigerator 20 minutes before cooking and to allow it to come to room temperature.

3. Preheat a grill or grill pan over high heat. Grill the chicken breasts until thoroughly cooked, 5 to 7 minutes on each side; the meat should be solid white throughout and the internal temperature should be 165°F.

4. Serve hot with the lemon wedges.

note: If your kitchen doesn't have a hood strong enough to take away the smoke a grill pan will generate, make the chicken in the broiler. Preheat the broiler and place the chicken breasts on an oiled, flameproof dish. Place chicken under the broiler and cook 4 to 5 minutes a side. The breasts should feel springy to the touch.

Nariyal ke Saath Murg

CHICKEN IN COCONUT & PEANUT CURRY

The Thai-inspired addition of coconut milk and peanuts to a traditional chicken curry makes for a rich, deliciously creamy and hearty dish. My friend Jan who lives in Germany wrote to me recently and said that he made this recipe with 1/4 cup peanut butter in place of the raw peanuts and much preferred it that way. Who am I to argue with Jan? He is an outstanding cook and loves all things Indian. | serves 4

1 (13 1/2-ounce) can unsweetened coconut milk

1/2 cup raw, skinless peanuts

4 boneless, skinless chicken breasts (about 2 pounds), cut into 1-inch pieces

1/2 teaspoon salt

1/2 teaspoon freshly ground black pepper

1/4 cup vegetable oil

2 medium red onions, finely chopped

3 tablespoons minced garlic

3 tablespoons peeled, minced fresh ginger

2 fresh green chile peppers (such as serrano), finely chopped

4 green cardamom pods, lightly crushed

1/2 cup chicken stock

Basmati rice (page 78), for serving

1. In a blender, finely purée 1/2 cup coconut milk with the peanuts until smooth. Combine with the remaining coconut milk and set aside.

2. Season the chicken with salt and pepper. Heat the oil in a large, deep skillet or Dutch oven over medium-high heat and stir-fry the seasoned chicken in batches just until lightly golden, 2 to 3 minutes per batch. Depending on the size of your pan you will have to do this in 2 to 3 batches so as not to overcrowd the chicken. Remove with a slotted spoon to a bowl and keep warm.

3. Sauté the onions in the same pan until softened, about 5 minutes. Add the garlic, ginger, green chiles, and cardamom. Stir-fry until the spices become aromatic, 1 to 2 minutes.

4. Add the reserved chicken pieces, along with the coconut milk mixture and chicken stock. Slowly bring to a boil, stirring frequently. Reduce the heat to low and gently simmer, uncovered, until chicken is fully cooked, about 10 minutes. Be careful to keep the curry at a very low simmer or the coconut milk will separate. Adjust the seasoning with salt and pepper to taste, and serve hot with basmati rice, if desired.

Murg Tellicherry

CHICKEN WITH TELLICHERRY PEPPER & CARAMELIZED ONIONS

2 tablespoons olive oil
2 medium red onions, sliced thinly and separated into rings
2 tablespoons vegetable oil
1 teaspoon cumin seeds
1 teaspoon garam masala (page 25)
2 pounds boneless, skinless chicken breast, cut into 1-inch pieces
10 fresh curry leaves
One 2-inch long cinnamon stick, broken in half
2 green cardamom pods, lightly crushed
1 tablespoon ground coriander
1 teaspoon ground cumin
1 teaspoon salt
2 tablespoons freshly ground Tellicherry peppercorns
Cilantro Chutney (page 49), for serving

This variation on *biryani*, a rice dish with chicken, Tellicherry peppercorns, and fried onions, is inspired by meals shared with my brother while I was in college. My brother would take me out to eat at a restaurant in Mumbai. We always ordered *biryani*—my brother would eat all the rice, leaving behind the chicken and onions for me. This recipe represents my favorite part of the dish and omits the rice (you won't miss it). Instead of frying the onions, I caramelize them—the sweetness complements the unique flavor of the Tellicherry peppercorns. | serves 4

1. Heat the olive oil in a medium skillet over medium heat. Add the onions and cook, stirring occasionally, until caramelized, 15 to 20 minutes, adding 1 tablespoon of water at a time if the onions begin to stick. Set aside.

2. Heat the vegetable oil in a large, nonstick saucepan with a lid over medium-high heat. Add the cumin seeds and garam masala; brown for about 2 minutes. Add the chicken, curry leaves, cinnamon, cardamom, coriander, cumin, salt, and Tellicherry peppercorns. Increase the heat to high and pan sear the mixture, turning constantly, until browned, about 5 minutes. Reduce the heat to low and cook, tightly covered, until the chicken is cooked through but still tender, 5 to 7 minutes. Add a little water if the chicken begins to stick to the pan.

3. Serve hot, garnished with the caramelized onions and chutney on the side.

Batak Vindaloo

DUCK VINDALOO WITH PIRI PIRI PEPPERS

- 5 whole piri piri peppers, or any other hot chile peppers
- 1 teaspoon black peppercorns
- 1 teaspoon cumin seeds
- 1 teaspoon black mustard seeds
- 1 tablespoon peeled, minced fresh ginger
- 1 tablespoon minced garlic
- 1/2 teaspoon sugar
- 1/2 teaspoon salt
- 1/4 cup white vinegar
- 4 large (1-pound) Muscovy duck breasts, skin removed and discarded, cut into 1-inch pieces (see Note)
- 3 tablespoons vegetable oil
- 1 large red onion, minced
- 1/4 cup dry red wine

The term *vindaloo* is derived from the Portuguese dish carne de *vinha d'alhos*, a dish of meat (usually pork) with wine and garlic. Today this dish has its own style and has become a Goan specialty, often served on special occasions. In this version, I use piri piri peppers which are widely used in Portuguese cuisine. You can substitute these with any other hot pepper. | serves 4

1. In a blender, combine the peppers, peppercorns, cumin seeds, mustard seeds, ginger, garlic, sugar, salt, and vinegar and blend into a paste. Place the spice paste in a large bowl and add the duck; mix to coat the meat. Cover and refrigerate for 4 to 6 hours.

2. Heat the oil in a wide, heavy skillet with a lid over medium heat. Add the onion and sauté until tender and lightly browned, about 5 minutes. Add all the duck pieces, reserving any excess marinade, and sauté until the duck is browned on all sides. Add the reserved marinade and the wine. Bring to a boil, then cover and reduce the heat to low. Simmer until the duck is tender and thoroughly cooked, 10 to 12 minutes. Serve hot.

note: Duck breasts come as one butterflied breast. You will have to slice down the middle to separate them. The best ducks are Muscovy ducks, available from specialty butchers, but any duck will work.

Murg Roshan

CHICKEN & RICOTTA CHEESE CURRY

Many of my regular guests find this creamy curry with dense ricotta cheese addictive. If you want to reduce the calories, substitute lowfat yogurt for the heavy cream. To avoid curdling the yogurt in the hot pan, add it very slowly, just a little at a time, and don't allow the sauce to boil. | serves 4 to 6

2 tablespoons ghee or vegetable oil

2 pounds boneless, skinless chicken breast, cut into 1-inch chunks

6 green cardamom pods

One 1-inch-long piece cinnamon stick

2 medium red onions, finely chopped

4 dried red chile peppers

One 2-inch-long piece fresh ginger, peeled and finely chopped

3 teaspoons ground turmeric

2 tablespoons dried fenugreek leaves

1 cup fresh ricotta cheese

1/2 teaspoon salt

1 cup heavy cream or lowfat yogurt

1/4 cup plain, lowfat yogurt, whisked smooth

1/4 cup golden raisins

4 fresh mint sprigs, for garnish

Basmati rice (page 78), for serving

1. Heat the ghee or oil in a large saucepan over medium-high heat and stir-fry the chicken in batches just until lightly golden, about 2 minutes. Remove with a slotted spoon.

2. To the same saucepan add the cardamom, cinnamon, onions, red chiles, ginger, turmeric, and fenugreek leaves. Stir-fry until the spices become aromatic and the onions become soft, 1 to 2 minutes. Add the ricotta cheese and salt and cook, stirring constantly, until well combined. Add the chicken, heavy cream, yogurt, and raisins and slowly bring to a brisk simmer, stirring occasionally. Reduce heat to low and simmer gently, uncovered, until the chicken pieces are cooked, about 10 minutes.

3. Adjust the salt to taste and garnish with mint sprigs. Serve with basmati rice.

MEAT

Considering the variety of religions practiced in India, many with dietary restrictions, it is little wonder that goat became the meat of choice. It also helps that goats are sturdy animals and require little grazing land. In the U.S., lamb is used as the main ingredient, although beef or pork can work just as well.

• • •

As with many styles of rustic cooking, Indian cuisine typically uses meat cooked on the bone for added flavor. The dishes in this section are infused with a variety of spices and seasonings and are simmered slowly over low heat, allowing the flavors to penetrate the meat. Whether using bone-in or boneless meat, these dishes will have rich flavor.

LAMB IN VINEGAR AND BEET CURRY

STAR ANISE–CRUSTED RACK OF LAMB

HOME-STYLE LAMB CURRY

BRUSSELS SPROUTS AND LAMB IN CASHEW AND ONION SAUCE

STEWED LAMB WITH CHANTERELLE MUSHROOMS

GARAM MASALA–CRUSTED ROASTED LEG OF LAMB

CARDAMOM-FLAVORED LAMB SHANK WITH CARAMELIZED ONIONS

BAY LEAF AND CUMIN–SCENTED GROUND LAMB

A Farewell Meal

I graduated from Welcomgroup still hungry for more knowledge. Though I returned home to Amritsar for a short while, I knew I must keep growing and testing myself. For me, that meant going to a culinary capital like New York or London. Without being able to say why, I knew it had to be New York.

Everyone who leaves home to emigrate to a new place must feel the same sense of thrill and fear, anticipation and nerves. I certainly felt it. As the date of my departure approached, I felt as if I were jumping out of my own skin and my mind wouldn't settle.

To calm myself, I went to the place I always went when I needed to feel centered: the Golden Temple in Amritsar. It is a Sikh temple, the most holy one in the world, and their spirit of sharing and fellowship gives me a powerful sense of belonging and rootedness. The Langar at the Golden Temple is a magnificent place where people from all classes, both Sikh and non-Sikh, gather for free communal meals. Volunteer devotees bring food to cook and serve, sharing a sense of community with the world.

My mother and I sat together quietly on the floor of the temple and enjoyed one last meal together, talking occasionally about the future, and my mind was calmed. Having a sense of home is important to me—while I knew I was heading to a new world, a part of me would always remain behind.

Chukandri Gosht

LAMB IN VINEGAR & BEET CURRY

I love lamb and am always looking to do something different with it. This unique sweet and tart curry gets its natural sweetness from beets, which are highly nutritious and give the dish a striking red color. I love blanching the beet tops, known as beet spinach, in boiling water and serving them under grilled meats. Fresh beets are a must for true flavor. The amount of vinegar can be reduced for a less tart dish. Serve this dish with any of the Indian breads or rice dishes. | serves 6

- 3 tablespoons vegetable oil
- 1 large red onion, finely chopped
- 2 tablespoons finely chopped garlic
- Two 2-inch-long cinnamon sticks
- 6 green cardamom pods
- 3 bay leaves
- 2 pounds lean boneless lamb, preferably leg of lamb, cut into 1-inch cubes
- 3 tablespoons white vinegar
- 1/3 cup tomato paste
- 4 medium beets, peeled and cut into 1-inch cubes
- 2 cups chicken stock
- 1 cup heavy cream
- Salt
- 1/2 cup finely chopped fresh cilantro

1. Heat the oil in a large, heavy-bottom pan with a lid over medium heat. Add the onion and cook until translucent, about 3 minutes. Add the garlic, cinnamon, cardamom, and bay leaves and cook, stirring, until fragrant, 1 to 2 minutes.

2. Add the lamb and cook, stirring, for 2 minutes; add the vinegar, tomato paste, beets, and chicken stock and mix well. Bring to a boil and reduce the heat to low. Cover and simmer until the lamb is tender, about 1 hour. Check occasionally to make sure it doesn't get too dry and stick to the bottom; add a little water if needed.

3. Add the cream and let it simmer 5 minutes. Discard the bay leaves. Season with salt to taste, add the cilantro, and mix well. Serve hot.

Anarphal Burrah

STAR ANISE-CRUSTED RACK OF LAMB

The leg and rack are the most tender cuts on a lamb. Ask your butcher to "french" the bones, i.e., to scrape off the excess fat from the exposed bones. This will help make the lamb look clean and appealing. The key to a juicy, tender rack of lamb is to sear it in a hot pan which will create a perfect crust and help hold in the juices. The star anise gives the lamb a warm, woody flavor. One rack is usually enough for two people and is best served rare to medium-rare. This dish goes well with a variety of chutneys. I recommend Blueberry Chutney with Orange Zest. | serves 4

- 2 (12- to 14-ounce), racks of lamb, frenched
- 8 whole star anise
- 8 long black peppers or black peppercorns
- 1 teaspoon salt
- 1/4 cup vegetable oil
- Blueberry Chutney with Orange Zest (page 34)

1. Preheat the oven to 400°F. Remove the lamb from the refrigerator 15 minutes before cooking. In a spice grinder or coffee grinder, blend the star anise and peppers to a fine powder. Generously rub the racks with salt and then the spice rub; let them sit for another 5 minutes.

2. Heat the oil in a heavy-bottom, ovenproof skillet. Sear the racks, fat side down, until very fragrant, about 5 minutes.

3. Place the skillet in the oven and bake the lamb until cooked as desired: 15 minutes for medium-rare; 20 minutes for medium. Serve with chutney.

- 3 medium red onions, chopped
- 1 tablespoon cayenne pepper
- 1 tablespoon ground cumin
- 1/2 tablespoon ground turmeric
- 1 1/2 cups plain, lowfat yogurt
- 2 teaspoons garam masala (page 25)
- 1/2 teaspoon salt
- 2 pounds boneless leg of lamb, cut into 1-inch cubes
- 3 tablespoons vegetable oil
- 5 green cardamom pods
- 3 bay leaves
- One 1-inch-long piece cinnamon stick
- 1 teaspoon cumin seeds
- 1 tablespoon ground coriander
- 4 fresh green chile peppers (such as serrano), minced
- 1 medium tomato, chopped
- 1 1/2 cups water
- 1/2 cup finely chopped fresh cilantro, for garnish
- Basmati rice (page 78), for serving

Ghar Jaisai Gosht Curry

HOME-STYLE LAMB CURRY

This classic North Indian dish is my all-time favorite curry. Whenever I cook it, the house fills with the wonderful aroma of lamb and spices. If this dish is made a day in advance, the flavors have time to develop and become even more delicious. You can substitute other meat or vegetables for the lamb and adjust the cooking time. Goat is chewier and requires more cooking time; beef needs less time. This dish tastes great served over basmati rice. | serves 6

1. In a blender or a food processor, blend together the onions, cayenne pepper, cumin, turmeric, 1/2 cup yogurt, garam masala, and salt.

2. In a large bowl, combine the yogurt mixture and the lamb, making sure all the pieces are well coated with the marinade. Cover with plastic wrap and marinate in the refrigerator for at least 4 hours, but no more than 6 hours.

3. Heat the oil in a large, nonstick saucepan over medium-high heat; add the cardamom, bay leaves, cinnamon, and cumin seeds. They should sizzle upon contact with the hot oil. Quickly add the coriander; mix in the marinated lamb and sauté over high heat, stirring, for 5 minutes. Reduce the heat to medium-low, cover the pan, and cook until most of the juices are dry, 15 to 20 minutes.

4. Add the green chiles, tomato, water, and the remaining yogurt and bring to a boil over high heat. Reduce the heat to medium-low, cover the pan, and simmer until the lamb is tender and the sauce is thick, about 10 more minutes. Discard the bay leaves.

5. Garnish with cilantro and serve hot with basmati rice.

Kaju- Pyaaz Gosht

BRUSSELS SPROUTS & LAMB IN CASHEW & ONION SAUCE

Brussels sprouts are available year round; however, they are at their best from fall through early spring. Using sprout heads of roughly the same size ensures that they cook evenly. The hard, bright-green sprouts are the most flavorful ones. | serves 6

- 1 1/2 pounds boneless leg of lamb, cut into 1-inch cubes
- 1/2 teaspoon salt
- 1/4 cup vegetable oil
- 1 medium Spanish onion, sliced
- 10 whole cashews, plus 2 tablespoons coarsely chopped cashews
- 4 green cardamom pods
- One 2-inch-long cinnamon stick
- 6 whole peppercorns
- 1 1/2 cups water
- 1/2 cup plain, lowfat yogurt, whisked smooth
- 1/2 cup heavy cream
- 1 teaspoon ground cumin
- 1 teaspoon ground coriander
- 8 ounces Brussels sprouts, halved lengthwise
- Basmati rice (page 78) or bread, for serving

1. Generously season the lamb with salt and set it aside for 10 minutes. In a heavy-bottom pan with a lid, heat the oil over medium heat and sear the lamb in batches for 6 to 8 minutes, tossing every few minutes to brown evenly. Remove with a slotted spoon and drain on a kitchen towel.

2. To the same pan, add the onion and cook until soft, about 2 minutes. Add the whole cashews, cardamom, cinnamon, and peppercorns and cook until very fragrant, about 2 minutes. Add the lamb, water, yogurt, cream, cumin, and coriander and, stirring occasionally, bring to a simmer. Reduce the heat to low, cover, and simmer 10 minutes. Add the Brussels sprouts and continue to simmer until the lamb is tender and cooked, about 20 more minutes. Add a little more water as needed to maintain the consistency of a nice stew.

3. Garnish with chopped cashews and serve with rice or bread if desired.

- 2 red onions, chopped
- 4 cloves garlic, chopped
- 2 tablespoons peeled, roughly chopped fresh ginger
- 2 fresh green chile peppers (such as serrano)
- 2 tablespoons vegetable oil
- 2 bay leaves
- 2 pounds boneless leg of lamb, cut into 1-inch cubes
- 1 teaspoon cayenne pepper
- 2 tablespoons ground coriander
- 2 tablespoons ground cumin
- 1/4 teaspoon ground turmeric
- 1/2 teaspoon garam masala (page 25)
- 1 tablespoon tomato paste
- 2 tablespoons plain, lowfat yogurt
- 1/2 teaspoon salt
- 1 teaspoon freshly ground black pepper
- 1 1/2 cups water
- 1 pound golden chanterelle mushrooms, cleaned and halved lengthwise
- Basmati rice (page 78) or bread, for serving

Khumbh aur Ghosht ke Curry

STEWED LAMB WITH CHANTERELLE MUSHROOMS

Wild chanterelle mushrooms and lamb complement each other in this delicious dish. Golden chanterelles have the fruity aroma of apricots and their flavor can range from slightly peppery to intensely woodsy and nutty. Pan-roasting the meat helps retain its moisture and makes it juicy and tender. | serves 6

1. Place the onions, garlic, ginger, and green chiles in a blender and process to a paste. Heat the oil in a large skillet with a lid over medium-high heat and add the onion mixture and the bay leaves. Cook, stirring occasionally, 5 to 7 minutes. Add the meat and cook, stirring, until all the pieces are thoroughly coated with the onion mixture, about 15 minutes.

2. Add the cayenne pepper, coriander, cumin, turmeric, and garam masala and stir well. Cook for 1 to 2 minutes. Stir in the tomato paste and yogurt and season with salt and pepper. Pour in the water and bring to a boil, stirring occasionally. Reduce the heat to low, cover, and simmer for 30 minutes. Add the mushrooms and continue simmering, covered, until the lamb is tender and fully cooked, 20 to 25 minutes. Remove the lid and simmer uncovered for the last 5 minutes if the sauce is too thin. Adjust salt and pepper to taste. Serve hot with rice or bread.

Raan Masaledaar

GARAM MASALA-CRUSTED ROASTED LEG OF LAMB

- 1 (7-pound) semi-boneless leg of lamb, aitchbone removed, fat trimmed to 1/4-inch thick, and then tied with kitchen twine for roasting
- 8 cloves garlic
- One 2-inch-long piece fresh ginger, peeled and cut into 4 pieces
- 1 cup fresh cilantro leaves
- 1/4 cup fresh mint leaves
- 1/2 cup garam masala (page 25)
- Juice of 2 lemons
- 1/2 teaspoon salt
- 1 teaspoon freshly ground black pepper
- 1/2 cup olive oil, plus more for the roasting pan

Lamb pairs well with the garam masala and garlic-ginger rub in this recipe. Marinating the meat overnight brings out the best flavor, and letting it rest before carving allows the juices to spread throughout the meat. | serves 6

1. Pat the lamb dry and score the fat by making shallow cuts all over with the tip of a small, sharp knife.

2. Place the garlic, ginger, cilantro, mint, garam masala, lemon juice, salt, pepper, and oil in a food processor and process until smooth. Evenly rub the paste all over the lamb, wrap well, and refrigerate 6 hours or overnight.

3. Preheat the oven to 425°F. Remove lamb from the refrigerator and let stand at room temperature for 30 minutes. Place lamb on a lightly oiled rack in a roasting pan and roast on the middle rack of the oven for 20 minutes, then reduce heat to 350°F and cook until an instant-read thermometer inserted 2 inches into the thickest part of the meat (but not touching bone) registers 135°F, about 1 3/4 hours.

4. Transfer to a cutting board and let stand 15 to 20 minutes. Cut off the twine and slice the meat crosswise, against the grain.

Elaichiwala Lamb Shank

CARDAMOM-FLAVORED LAMB SHANK WITH CARAMELIZED ONIONS

Wonderfully tender, these lamb shanks melt in your mouth. Here, the shanks are slow-cooked in red wine and tomato sauce flavored with cardamom, cloves, and a host of other spices. Red wine gives it an intense, deep flavor. Spices add fragrance, and their flavors develop the longer they are cooked. Caramelized onions add the perfect finishing touch. | serves 4

4 (1 1/2-pound) lamb shanks

Salt and freshly ground black pepper

1/4 cup ghee

8 to 10 green cardamom pods

6 whole cloves

One 2-inch-long cinnamon stick

1 teaspoon whole black peppercorns

1 whole star anise

2 bay leaves

2 large Spanish onions, thinly sliced

2 tablespoons chopped garlic

One 2-inch-long piece fresh ginger, peeled and finely chopped

3 ribs celery, without leaves, finely chopped

2 medium tomatoes, finely chopped

2 tablespoons tomato paste

1 cup dry red wine, preferably Cabernet Sauvignon

Juice of 1 lemon

5 cups chicken broth

1 tablespoon olive oil

1 medium red onion, chopped

1. Preheat the oven to 300°F. Pat the lamb shanks dry with paper towels and season generously with salt and pepper. Let sit for 15 minutes.

2. Heat the ghee in a large Dutch oven over medium-high heat. Add the lamb shanks and evenly brown on all sides, 4 to 5 minutes per side. Transfer shanks to a plate, cover, and keep warm.

3. Add the cardamom, cloves, cinnamon, peppercorns, star anise, and bay leaves and stir continuously until the mixture is very fragrant, about 2 minutes. Add the Spanish onions, garlic, ginger, celery, tomatoes, and tomato paste and cook, stirring occasionally, until all the liquid is evaporated, 8 to 10 minutes. Add the red wine and stir continuously, scraping up any browned bits that cling to the bottom. Bring to a boil, then reduce heat to medium and cook until the wine is syrupy, about 5 minutes.

4. Add the lamb shanks, lemon juice, and chicken broth to the mixture and bring it to a boil. Remove from heat, cover the pot, and transfer it to the oven. Cook 1 1/2 to 2 hours, turning the shanks occasionally, until the meat is just falling off the bone. If necessary, add more water to prevent the shanks from drying out.

5. While the lamb is cooking, heat the olive oil in a large skillet over medium heat. Add the red onions and cook, stirring occasionally, until caramelized, 15 to 20 minutes. Add 1 tablespoon water if the onions begin to stick. Set aside to use as a garnish.

6. Remove the shanks to a serving platter and skim any accumulated fat off the sauce. Discard the bay leaves, adjust the salt and pepper to taste, and pour the sauce over the shanks. Serve hot, garnished with the caramelized red onions.

- 3 tablespoons vegetable oil
- 1 medium onion, finely chopped
- 6 cloves garlic, finely chopped
- One 2-inch-long piece fresh ginger, peeled and finely chopped
- 1 fresh green chile pepper (such as serrano), seeded and minced
- 8 green cardamom pods
- 5 bay leaves
- 1 1/2 pounds lean ground lamb
- 1 teaspoon salt
- 2 tablespoons ground cumin
- 2 tablespoons ground coriander
- 1 teaspoon ground turmeric
- 1 teaspoon paprika
- 1 medium tomato, blanched for 30 seconds, skinned, and finely chopped
- 1/2 cup plain, lowfat yogurt, whisked smooth
- 1 cup water
- 1/4 cup almond slivers
- Basmati rice (page 78) or bread, for serving

Jeera Keema

BAY LEAVES & CUMIN-SCENTED GROUND LAMB

This popular Indian recipe, also called *keema* (which literally means 'ground meat'), can be made with any ground meat. A health-conscious cook might try it with ground turkey. In this version, ground lamb is sautéed with aromatic bay leaves, cumin, and cardamom and garnished with almonds. Other variations include additions such as peas and potatoes. | serves 4

1. Heat the oil in a medium, heavy-bottom skillet over medium-high heat and fry the onion until soft, about 3 minutes. Add the garlic, ginger, green chile, cardamom, and bay leaves and cook, stirring continuously, until the mixture is light brown, about 2 minutes.

2. Add the lamb, salt, cumin, coriander, turmeric, paprika, and tomato and cook, stirring and breaking up the lamb, until dry, about 2 minutes. Stir in the yogurt and water, reduce the heat to low, and simmer, stirring occasionally until the lamb is cooked, about 10 minutes. Add more water if necessary, to keep the dish from becoming too dry. Discard the bay leaves.

3. Serve hot, garnished with almonds, with rice or bread.

Christmas in New York

When I first left India to come to New York, I experienced major culture shock. I knew very few people, was often lonely for home, and everything seemed strange. My catering experience in India did not count in New York, so I had to work my way up from the bottom again.

My first Christmas in New York was memorable. I had no phone and only three dollars, just enough to get me to work and back. I knew if I went to work, I would be fed, so I made my way through the slushy snow, spending half my money on subway fare. I arrived to find the restaurant closed for the holiday. Not knowing what to do, I wandered around downtown. After passing many closed storefronts, I came upon a line of people. When I found out that they were waiting for a meal, I joined the line, thus spending my first Christmas at the New York Rescue Mission.

I didn't realize that such places existed in the United States. It reminded me of the Golden Temple in my hometown of Amritsar where people volunteer in the communal kitchen to feed hundreds of thousands of people every day. That first Christmas, I took my turn cooking and serving at the mission. The food was unfamiliar but the sense of community was the same as back home. It was a warm reminder that we are all connected by food and I knew then I would be okay in my new home.

SEAFOOD

One of my earliest memories of Mumbai is of visiting my brother and sampling seafood dishes that were all new to me. We didn't eat much seafood in the state of Punjab, but I feel that discovering seafood later in life has made me much more appreciative of it.

• • •

Seafood offers great variety in texture and flavor, from shellfish like prawns and mussels, to sea bass and salmon. The recipes in this section reflect this variety and showcase styles of preparation from throughout India. Be sure to use the freshest ingredients, as it will make all the difference.

FENUGREEK-SCENTED WHOLE RED SNAPPER

RED PEPPER AND PISTACHIO CURRIED SHRIMP

CLAMS IN MANGO CHUTNEY

BENGALI-STYLE FISH IN YOGURT CURRY

BANANA LEAF–WRAPPED SALMON WITH MINT-BASIL CHUTNEY

WHOLE SEA BASS STUFFED WITH RAISINS, CASHEWS, AND PISTACHIOS

PANCH PHORAN SHRIMP

MUSSELS IN GARLIC BUTTER, ASAFETIDA, AND WHITE WINE

KERALA FISHERMAN'S SQUID CURRY

LEMON AND FENNEL-CRUSTED SOLE

SHRIMP IN RED CURRY SAUCE

GRILLED SEA BASS WITH GOAN SPICE PASTE

CRAB IN COCONUT AND MADRAS CURRY

New Cuisines

Once in New York, I had to start at the bottom, bussing tables and washing dishes. Whenever I had money to spare, I spent it on learning more about food. I went to restaurants I could not afford and endured the surly stares of waiters who were doomed to the meager tips I could provide. (As soon as I began to make decent wages, I tipped very heavily to make up for it.) I saved all the money I didn't spend in restaurants and used it to further my culinary education, taking classes at NYU, Cornell, and the Culinary Institute of America. I attended workshops, bought cookbooks, and read restaurant reviews, methodically adding to my store of knowledge. I was stunned by the freedom and creativity of French and American chefs, while delighted by the clarity and delicious simplicity of Italian cuisine. Chinese cuisine turned out to be something rather different from what I knew and also highly regional, just like my native Indian cuisine.

Then there were the great Moroccan, Ethiopian, Greek, Mexican, Spanish, Japanese, Middle Eastern, Vietnamese, Thai, and American places. Each one of these cuisines has its own distinctive sense of aesthetics and I learned to evaluate my own cooking in light of the great wealth of beliefs and ideas about food that I was now faced with.

Indian cuisine is an incredibly rich, but limiting tradition. Our dishes have been perfected over several thousand years, and as a rule, creativity has never been encouraged or rewarded. Only recently are we beginning to break out of our traditions. My creative process now involves a new vocabulary full of words I never imagined and could have only learned here in New York. The new "World Cuisine" that was taking shape in New York and across the United States opened my eyes as nothing before. I was introduced to miraculous new ingredients that I had never heard of and could barely pronounce. There were fusion cuisines springing forth in a profusion of creativity.

Though some may fear that the creativity will go too far, resulting in a soulless and superficial cuisine, we must remember that we are also inventing new traditions. It took many centuries for the great cuisines of the world to evolve and what we are doing now will undergo its own process of revision many times over. For now, I am enjoying the exuberance and I'm delighted to be part of it.

Methi Machhi

FENUGREEK-SCENTED WHOLE RED SNAPPER

Red snapper has beautiful red and pink colors in its skin, and its firm white flesh has a slightly sweet flavor that is highlighted by the spices in this dish. | serves 4

- 1 tablespoon ground coriander
- 1 tablespoon curry powder (page 23)
- 1 tablespoon ground cumin
- 1/2 teaspoon ground turmeric
- 1 teaspoon caraway seeds
- 1 tablespoon garam masala (page 25)
- 2 tablespoons finely chopped fresh cilantro
- 2 teaspoons salt
- 1/4 cup dried fenugreek leaves
- 4 (1-pound) whole red snappers, scaled and gutted
- 1 lemon
- 2 tablespoons vegetable oil
- 2 tablespoons ghee

1. In a large mixing bowl, combine the coriander, curry powder, cumin, turmeric, caraway seeds, garam masala, cilantro, salt, and fenugreek leaves.

2. Wash the fish thoroughly under cold running water and dry well with paper towels. With a sharp knife make 4 to 6 vertical gashes, 2 1/2-inches long, on each side. Cut the lemon into quarters and squeeze it over the fish, then gently rub the spice mixture inside and outside the fish. Cover and let marinate in the refrigerator for 2 to 4 hours. Remove the fish from the refrigerator 15 to 20 minutes before cooking.

3. Preheat the oven to 300°F. Evenly grease a baking dish with the vegetable oil. Heat a large skillet over high heat and add the ghee. Sauté the fish, browning it nicely on both sides, about 3 minutes per side. As each fish is browned, lay it in the baking dish.

4. Place the baking dish in the oven and bake until the fish is cooked (it flakes easily with a fork), about 15 minutes. Serve hot.

Shimla Mirch Curry Jhinga

RED PEPPER & PISTACHIO CURRIED SHRIMP

- 1 large red bell pepper, coarsely chopped
- 1 large red onion, coarsely chopped
- 1/2 cup raw, shelled pistachios, plus 10 finely chopped pistachios for garnish
- 2 fresh green chile peppers (such as serrano)
- 1/2 cup water
- 4 tablespoons vegetable oil
- 1 tablespoon cumin seeds
- 1 tablespoon finely chopped garlic
- 1 pound medium shrimp, shelled and deveined
- 1/2 teaspoon salt
- 1/2 cup heavy cream
- 1/4 cup chopped fresh mint leaves

There are never any leftovers when I serve this creamy shrimp dish. The sweetness of the red peppers blends with red onions, cumin, garlic, and green chiles. Pistachios are ideal, though you can substitute your favorite nuts. It is typical in Indian cooking to use raw nuts rather than toasted as in the West. You can, of course, use toasted nuts, but the flavor will be less authentic. | serves 4

1. In a blender or a food processor blend the bell pepper, onion, pistachios, green chiles, and water into a smooth purée.

2. In a medium skillet, heat 3 tablespoons of the oil over medium heat. Add the cumin seeds and cook for 1 minute, stirring. Add the garlic and cook until the edges turn brown, about 1 minute. Add the shrimp and salt and cook until just opaque, 2 to 3 minutes. Remove shrimp from the pan with a slotted spoon and drain on a paper towel.

3. Add the remaining tablespoon oil to the same skillet, gently add the red pepper mixture and cream, and bring to a boil. Reduce heat to low and simmer the sauce for 5 minutes to cook the onion. Add the shrimp and simmer for another 3 to 4 minutes. Stir in the chopped mint just before serving to preserve its fresh flavor.

4. Season with salt to taste and serve hot, topped with the remaining chopped pistachios.

Tisario Aam Chutney ke saath

CLAMS IN MANGO CHUTNEY

- 1 cup Mango-Lemon Chutney (page 43)
- 1 cup plain, whole-milk yogurt
- 1/4 cup coarsely chopped fresh cilantro
- Salt and freshly ground black pepper
- 4 tablespoons unsalted butter
- 2 tablespoons chopped garlic
- 24 clams (about 2 pounds) in the shell, well scrubbed
- Juice of 1 lemon

Plump littleneck clams are best for this recipe, as they have the most flavor. Yogurt-based mango chutney adds an interesting twist. Served with some warm crusty bread for dipping, this is one of my favorite light meals. | serves 4

1. In a blender, purée the mango-lemon chutney, yogurt, and cilantro until smooth. Season with salt and pepper to taste.

2. In a large pot with a tight-fitting lid, melt the butter over medium heat, add the garlic, and stir until golden brown, about 2 minutes. Add the clams and pour the yogurt chutney over them evenly. Cover the pan with the lid and let the clams steam for about 5 minutes, or until all the shells have opened. Discard any clams that do not open.

3. Squeeze the lemon juice over the clams before serving.

Bengali Dahi Maach

BENGALI-STYLE FISH IN YOGURT CURRY

Tender pieces of tilapia are marinated with caraway seeds, turmeric, and cayenne pepper and then pan-fried until crisp and golden brown. The dish is finished with a yogurt curry enhanced by the spicy flavor of mustard seeds. The result is a great mixture of flavors and textures, and a simple way to prepare versatile tilapia. | serves 4

- 1/2 teaspoon ground turmeric
- 1/2 teaspoon freshly ground black pepper
- 1/2 teaspoon cayenne pepper
- 1/2 teaspoon caraway seeds
- 1 pound tilapia fillets, cut into 1- to 2-inch pieces
- 1 cup plain, lowfat yogurt
- 1 tablespoon all-purpose flour
- 5 tablespoons vegetable oil
- 1 tablespoon black mustard seeds
- 1 medium red onion, finely chopped
- 1 tablespoon finely chopped garlic
- 1 tablespoon curry powder (page 23)
- 1 1/4 cups heavy cream
- Salt
- 2 tablespoons finely chopped fresh cilantro, for garnish

1. Mix together the turmeric, black pepper, cayenne pepper, and caraway seeds. Add the tilapia pieces and toss to coat. Cover and let sit for 30 minutes in the refrigerator.

2. In a blender, combine the yogurt and flour and set aside. Heat 3 tablespoons of the oil in a medium skillet over medium-high heat. Add the mustard seeds and cook, stirring, until sputtering and fragrant, about 1 minute. Add the onion and cook, stirring, until translucent, about 3 minutes. Add the garlic and curry powder and cook for another 2 minutes. Add the cream and the yogurt mixture and bring to a simmer. Reduce the heat to low and simmer until the sauce is thick, about 5 minutes.

3. In a nonstick pan, heat the remaining 2 tablespoons oil over medium heat. Gently fry the seasoned fish until crisp on both sides, about 3 minutes per side. Add the yogurt mixture to the fried fish and simmer until fish is cooked through, about 5 minutes.

4. Season with salt to taste and serve hot, garnished with fresh cilantro.

Patra-ni-Macchi

BANANA LEAF-WRAPPED SALMON WITH MINT-BASIL CHUTNEY

- 1/2 cup packed fresh basil leaves
- 1/2 cup packed fresh mint leaves
- 2 cloves garlic
- 1 cup raw cashews
- 2 fresh hot green chile peppers (such as Thai or serrano)
- 1/4 cup water
- Juice of 1 lemon
- 1/4 cup olive oil
- Salt
- 2 pounds thick, skinless salmon fillets, cut into 12 equal pieces
- 1 large banana leaf, cut into 12 equal-size squares (available at flower shops or Caribbean groceries), or aluminum foil

This recipe, inspired by my days of living as a tenant with a Parsi family in Bombay, is extremely popular in the Parsi community. Pomfret is usually used in this recipe, but in my version, I use salmon. | serves 6

1. Preheat the oven to 300°F. To make the chutney, place the basil, mint, garlic, cashews, chiles, water, and lemon juice in a blender or a food processor; pulse, drizzling in the olive oil, until it forms a coarse paste, scraping down the sides as necessary. The paste will be very thick.

2. Gently cut a deep horizontal slit in the side of each salmon fillet (don't cut through completely). Season the fillets lightly with salt. Fill each slit with 1 teaspoon basil-mint chutney. Evenly divide the remainder of the chutney on top of the fillets.

3. Place each piece of fish on a banana leaf or piece of aluminum foil, wrapping it in the leaf or foil as you would a parcel. If using banana leaves, tie with kitchen string. Place the parcels on a nonstick baking sheet and bake until the fish is cooked through, about 20 minutes. Serve hot.

Kishmish-Pista Maach

WHOLE SEA BASS STUFFED WITH RAISINS, CASHEWS & PISTACHIOS

4 whole sea bass (1 to 1 1/2 pounds each), scaled and gutted

Juice of 1 lemon, 1 tablespoon reserved

1 teaspoon salt

1/2 cup golden raisins, plumped for 15 minutes in 2 cups of hot water and then drained

1/2 cup cashews, coarsely chopped

1/4 cup shelled, raw pistachios, coarsely chopped

1 medium tomato, seeded and coarsely chopped

One 2-inch-long piece fresh ginger, peeled and finely chopped

2 tablespoons finely chopped garlic

1/4 teaspoon freshly grated nutmeg

1 teaspoon ground cumin

2 tablespoons finely chopped fresh cilantro

2 medium carrots, cut into 1/2-inch diagonals

2 tablespoons olive oil

4 lemon slices

This recipe comes from my friend Chef Amita, whom I met while I was doing hotel management training in Delhi. During the slow afternoons we would sneak into the kitchen and experiment with the large variety of ingredients available. This dish is one of the recipes she put together. The fish is stuffed with raisins, cashews, pistachios, nutmeg, and garlic. The marinade in this recipe is light and does not overpower the flavors of the fish, and the crust that forms on the baked fish is delicious. | serves 4

1. With a sharp knife, make 4 to 6 vertical gashes, 2 to 2 1/2 inches long, on each side of the fish. Gently rub each fish inside and out with 1 tablespoon lemon juice and 1/2 teaspoon salt. Cover and marinate in the refrigerator for 2 to 6 hours.

2. In a large mixing bowl, combine the raisins, cashews, pistachios, tomato, ginger, garlic, nutmeg, remaining lemon juice, cumin, and cilantro. Cover and set aside.

3. Preheat the oven to 300°F. Evenly stuff the nut mixture into the gashes of the fish. Reserve any leftover nut mixture.

4. Toss the carrots with olive oil and remaining 1/2 teaspoon salt and spread them evenly on a rimmed baking sheet. Lay the lemon slices on top of the carrots then place the stuffed fish on top, layering the remaining nut mixture on top. Bake until the fish is cooked and it flakes easily with a fork, 30 to 35 minutes.

5. Serve garnished with the baked carrots and lemon slices.

- 2 tablespoons vegetable oil
- 1 tablespoon *panch phoran* spice mix (page 28)
- 1 pound medium shrimp, shelled and deveined
- 2 tablespoons dried fenugreek leaves
- 3 tablespoons tomato paste
- 1 red bell pepper, cut into 1-inch dice
- 1 green bell pepper, cut into 1-inch dice
- 1 yellow bell pepper, cut into 1-inch dice
- 1 medium red onion, cut into 1-inch dice
- Juice of 1 lemon
- 1 teaspoon cayenne pepper
- 1/4 cup water
- Pinch of salt
- Fresh chives, for garnish

Jhinga Paanch Phoron

PANCH PHORAN SHRIMP

Plump, succulent shrimp are combined here with *panch phoran*, a traditional Bengali spice mix. It is a blend of five spices: fenugreek, nigella seed, mustard seed, fennel seed, and cumin, and lends a lovely aroma to any dish, whether meat, fish, or vegetable. | serves 4

1. Heat the oil in a large skillet over medium heat. Add the *panch phoran* spice mix and cook until fragrant, about 1 minute. Add the shrimp and cook, stirring, for 2 to 3 minutes. Remove the shrimp from the pan with a slotted spoon and drain on a paper towel.

2. To the same skillet, add the fenugreek leaves, tomato paste, bell peppers, onion, lemon juice, cayenne pepper, water, and salt. Cook, stirring, until the onion softens, 4 to 5 minutes. Add the shrimp and mix until well coated.

3. Serve hot, garnished with fresh chives.

Hing-Lassan Teesari

MUSSELS IN GARLIC BUTTER, ASAFETIDA & WHITE WINE

- 4 tablespoons unsalted butter
- 4 cloves garlic, finely chopped
- 2 medium shallots, coarsely chopped
- 1 pinch ground asafetida
- 1/2 cup white wine
- 1/2 cup water
- 1 cup heavy cream
- Salt and freshly ground black pepper
- 2 pounds cultivated mussels, scrubbed (see Note)
- 2 tablespoons chopped fresh cilantro, for garnish

At a catering event in the Hamptons one year, I created a seafood-centered menu; for the mussels I made a light sauce of garlic, butter, and wine. The addition of asafetida enhances the sweet, briny flavor of the shellfish. | serves 4

1. Heat 2 tablespoons butter in a stockpot over medium heat. Add the garlic, shallots, and asafetida and cook until the shallots soften, about 3 minutes. Increase the heat to high, add the wine, and let it cook down to a syrup, about 4 minutes. Add the water, cream, and a pinch of salt and pepper; bring to a boil and stir in the mussels. Reduce the heat to medium, cover the pot with a tight-fitting lid, and cook until the mussels have opened, 6 to 8 minutes. Discard any mussels that do not open. Remove the mussels with a slotted spoon to a large bowl. Bring the cooking liquid to a simmer and whisk in the remaining 2 tablespoons butter. Adjust the salt and pepper to taste.

2. Pour the sauce over the mussels and serve immediately, garnished with cilantro.

note: Cultivated mussels are raised under controlled conditions. Harvesting wild mussels can damage fish eco-systems: use cultivated mussels whenever possible.

Samundar Pheni Curry

KERALA FISHERMAN'S SQUID CURRY

To keep squid tender and not rubbery, it is often either braised slowly or briefly cooked over high heat. In this recipe, we do the latter: the calamari is simmered for just a few minutes in a sweet and spicy curry. This is a specialty from Kerala, known as "the land of the backwaters," located on the southwestern coast of India. | serves 6

- 1 teaspoon cumin seeds
- 1 teaspoon coriander seeds
- 1 teaspoon fennel seeds
- 2 teaspoons cayenne pepper
- 1 teaspoon ground turmeric
- 2 pounds fresh squid, cleaned and cut into 1-inch rings
- 1 tablespoon chopped scallions
- Salt
- 2 tablespoons vegetable oil
- 10 fresh curry leaves
- 4 cloves garlic, crushed
- 2 tablespoons peeled, minced fresh ginger
- 2 red onions, thinly sliced
- 1 (13 1/2-ounce) can unsweetened coconut milk
- 1/2 cup heavy cream
- 1 tablespoon fresh lime juice

1. In a small frying pan over low heat, dry-roast (see page 17) the cumin, coriander, and fennel seeds until aromatic, about 1 minute. In a spice grinder, grind the seed mixture, cayenne pepper, and turmeric to a fine powder.

2. In a medium bowl, toss the squid and the scallions with a pinch of salt; set aside for 10 minutes.

3. In a heavy-bottom frying pan, heat the oil over medium-high heat. Add the curry leaves, garlic, and ginger and sauté for 1 minute, stirring constantly. Add the onions and spice mix and sauté until lightly browned, 4 to 5 minutes. Add the coconut milk and heavy cream. Bring to a boil then reduce the heat to low and simmer for 2 to 3 minutes. Add the squid and scallions and simmer just until the squid is cooked through and tender, 5 to 6 minutes.

4. Stir in the lime juice, season with salt to taste, and serve.

Nimboo-Saunf Maach

LEMON & FENNEL-CRUSTED SOLE

- 2 pounds firm fish fillets (such as skinless sole or flounder), cut into 3-inch pieces
- 2 teaspoons salt
- 1 tablespoon fresh lemon juice
- 1/3 cup rice flour
- 2 teaspoons cayenne pepper
- 1 teaspoon ground fennel
- 2 cups vegetable oil, for deep-frying
- Lemon wedges, for garnish

Rice flour is the secret ingredient that makes this recipe a success. It gives the fish a light, crispy crust. If you can't find rice flour, I've also used cornstarch with great results. | serves 6

1. Place the fish pieces on a large platter. Sprinkle with the salt and lemon juice and marinate about 30 minutes, covered with plastic wrap, in the refrigerator.

2. Mix the rice flour, cayenne pepper, and ground fennel in a medium mixing bowl. With a paper towel, dry each piece of fish, and then dredge it in the rice flour mixture.

3. Line a sheet pan with paper towels. Heat the oil in a large, nonstick skillet over medium-high heat until it reaches 350°F on a deep-fry thermometer. To test the oil, place a small cube of bread in the pan. The bread should sizzle on contact and brown immediately. Add a few pieces of fish at a time to the oil and deep-fry until golden brown and crispy on both sides, 4 to 5 minutes, while gently turning them with a spatula. Transfer to lined sheet pan to drain. Continue until all the fish is cooked.

4. Serve hot, garnished with lemon wedges.

- 1 tablespoon vegetable oil
- 1 tablespoon peeled, chopped fresh ginger
- 3 cloves garlic, chopped
- 2 shallots, chopped
- 10 fresh curry leaves
- 1/4 cup Thai red curry paste
- 1 1/2 pounds medium shrimp, peeled and deveined
- 1 tablespoon soy sauce
- 2 tablespoons fresh lemon juice
- 2 tablespoons chopped dried red chile pepper
- 2 tablespoons minced fresh cilantro
- 1/4 cup plain, lowfat yogurt, whisked smooth
- Salt
- 2 tablespoons chopped scallions, white and green parts, for garnish

Jhinga Curry

SHRIMP IN RED CURRY SAUCE

Shrimp is paired here with lightly spiced red curry paste, soy sauce, lemon juice, and yogurt. Red curry paste is Thai in origin and is made with lemongrass, lime rind, cumin, coriander, and shrimp paste. | serves 6

1. Heat the oil in a wok or a large, heavy-bottom pan over high heat until very hot. Add the ginger, garlic, shallots, curry leaves, and curry paste and sauté for 1 minute. Add the shrimp and cook just until they start to turn pink, 2 to 3 minutes. Add the soy sauce, lemon juice, dried chiles, and cilantro and cook, stirring often, 2 minutes longer. Reduce the heat to medium and add the yogurt. Cook until the shrimp are just cooked through, 2 minutes; season with salt to taste.

2. Serve warm, garnished with the chopped scallions.

- 1/2 cup plain, lowfat yogurt
- 2 tablespoons unsweetened coconut milk
- 1 tablespoon peeled, minced fresh ginger
- 1 tablespoon minced garlic
- 1 teaspoon red pepper flakes
- 3 tablespoons malt vinegar
- 2 teaspoons ground cumin
- 1/4 teaspoon ground cloves
- 1/2 teaspoon ground cinnamon
- 1 teaspoon paprika
- 1 teaspoon salt
- 2 pounds sea bass fillets, about 1 inch thick, cut into 2-inch pieces
- 1 tablespoon vegetable oil
- Lemon wedges, for garnish

Goan Macchli

GRILLED SEA BASS WITH GOAN SPICE PASTE

In this dish, sea bass is rubbed with *rechad masala*, a spice paste indispensable in the Indian region of Goa. It is most often used to stuff fish and other seafood, but in this recipe I have used the paste as a marinade before grilling, giving the fish a great smoky flavor. | serves 6

1. In a large bowl, combine all the ingredients except the fish, oil, and lemon wedges. Add the fish and toss, making sure all the pieces are well coated. Cover with plastic wrap and marinate in the refrigerator for 2 to 4 hours.

2. Heat the grill or grill pan over medium-high heat. Coat the grill or grill pan with oil to prevent the fish from sticking. Place the marinated fish on the grill and cook, turning once or twice, until the fish pieces are opaque and just flaky inside and lightly charred on the outside, 5 to 7 minutes.

3. Serve hot with lemon wedges.

- 2 tablespoons vegetable oil
- 1 teaspoon black mustard seeds
- 6 fresh curry leaves
- 1 medium red onion, finely chopped
- 6 to 8 scallions, finely chopped
- 1 red bell pepper, finely diced
- 1 tablespoon Madras curry powder (page 23)
- 1 pound jumbo lump crabmeat, picked over and cleaned
- 1/2 cup plain, lowfat yogurt, whisked smooth
- 1/2 cup unsweetened coconut milk
- 1/2 teaspoon salt
- 1/4 teaspoon freshly ground black pepper
- 2 tablespoons finely chopped fresh cilantro, for garnish

Madrasi Kekada

CRAB IN COCONUT & MADRAS CURRY

Madras curry is one of my all-time favorites. Its strong flavor mixes well with the crabmeat and is a crowd pleaser. Making it a day in advance helps develop the flavors and makes the curry taste even better. | serves 4

1. In a heavy-bottom skillet, heat the oil over medium heat. Add the mustard seeds and curry leaves and fry until the seeds begin to crackle, about 1 minute. Add the onion, scallions, red pepper, and curry powder and cook, stirring, until the ingredients are well mixed and the onion begins to brown on the edges, 5 to 6 minutes.

2. Stir in the crabmeat, yogurt, coconut milk, salt, and pepper. Turn the heat down to low and simmer until the sauce is thick and the crabmeat is cooked, about 5 minutes.

3. Adjust salt and pepper to taste, garnish with cilantro, and serve hot.

DESSERTS

Having worked with French and American chefs, my approach to desserts has become much more adventurous. I like to come up with new twists on the classics, such as a soufflé made out of basmati rice flour and chocolate chip cookies with candied rose petals.

...

In this section I've included a variety of desserts, from light and refreshing sorbets to compotes for topping your favorite cake. These will create the perfect ending to a meal—I believe how you end the meal is as important as how you start it.

BLOOD ORANGE AND STRAWBERRY SORBET

APPLE AND DATE COBBLER WITH CARDAMOM

CANDIED ROSE PETAL AND CHOCOLATE COOKIES

CHAI-INFUSED CRÈME BRÛLÉE

CHOCOLATE BASMATI RICE SOUFFLÉ

GULAB JAMUN WITH COCONUT FLAKES

MEYER LEMON AND GINGER COMPOTE

RICE CUSTARD WITH GOLDEN BERRIES AND HONEY

MANGO AND ORANGE MOUSSE WITH POMEGRANATE

PAN-SEARED PINEAPPLE WITH FENNEL CRÈME ANGLAISE

INDIAN RICE PUDDING WITH PISTACHIOS AND SILVER LEAVES

Santra aur Hisālū sorbet

BLOOD ORANGE & STRAWBERRY SORBET

- 2/3 cup water
- 2/3 cup sugar
- 3 cups fresh blood orange juice
- 2 cups fresh strawberries
- 2 tablespoons fresh lemon juice

This recipe requires a good quality ice-cream maker to achieve a smooth texture. If you have to substitute frozen strawberries for fresh, use the unsweetened ones. | serves 6

1. To make a simple syrup, place the water and sugar in a small saucepan over low heat and stir until the sugar is completely dissolved, 3 to 5 minutes. Bring the mixture to a boil and then remove from heat. Pour the sugar syrup into a heatproof container and place in the refrigerator until completely chilled, about 1 hour.

2. Place the blood orange juice and strawberries in a food processor and process until the strawberries are puréed. Transfer to a large bowl, stir in the lemon juice, and refrigerate until the mixture is thoroughly chilled, 30 minutes. Once the simple syrup and puréed strawberries are completely chilled, combine them.

3. Freeze the strawberry mixture in an ice-cream maker according to manufacturer's instructions. The sorbet will be soft but ready to eat. For a firmer sorbet, transfer the frozen sorbet to a freezer-safe container and freeze for at least 2 additional hours.

Seb ke saath Khajoor ka meetha

APPLE & DATE COBBLER WITH CARDAMOM

Serve this easy dessert in fall or winter, when apples are at their seasonal best. Vanilla or caramel ice cream makes an excellent accompaniment. | serves 4

- 3 to 4 ripe Fuji apples (1 1/4 pounds), peeled, cored, and cut into 1/4- to 1/2-inch dice
- 1 cup dates, pitted and coarsely chopped
- 1/4 cup plus 1 tablespoon sugar
- 1 teaspoon ground cardamom
- 2 teaspoons cornstarch
- 1 large egg
- 3 tablespoons unsalted butter, melted and cooled
- 1/4 cup heavy cream
- 1/2 cup plus 2 tablespoons all-purpose flour
- Pinch of salt
- 1 teaspoon baking powder

1. Preheat the oven to 350°F. Combine the apples and dates in a medium bowl. In a separate small bowl, whisk 1/4 cup sugar with the cardamom and cornstarch. Add to the apples and dates; toss to combine. Set aside.

2. Combine the egg, 2 tablespoons melted butter, and the cream in a bowl. Whisk with a fork. Set aside.

3. In a large bowl, sift together the flour, salt, baking powder, and remaining tablespoon sugar. Using your hands, slowly add the egg mixture, working it in until just combined. Divide the dough into 4 equal portions.

4. Divide the fruit mixture among four 8-ounce ramekins. Gently pat the dough into 4 disks just big enough to fit on top of the ramekins and drape the dough over the fruit without pressing down. Brush the tops with the remaining melted butter. Place the ramekins on a baking sheet and bake until juices bubble up and crust is golden brown, 15 to 17 minutes. Serve hot.

Gulkand ke Biskut

CANDIED ROSE PETAL & CHOCOLATE COOKIES

The all-American classic cookie has taken a detour to India in this recipe. The candied rose petals and dark, semisweet chocolate are divine together. Candied rose petals, known as *Gulkand* or rose spread, are available in Indian grocery stores. | makes 2 dozen cookies

12 tablespoons (1 1/2 sticks) unsalted butter

1 cup sugar

1/2 cup light brown sugar

1 large egg

1 egg yolk

2 tablespoons heavy cream

1/2 cup rose spread

2 1/4 cups all-purpose flour

1 teaspoon baking soda

1/2 teaspoon salt

2 cups finely chopped semisweet chocolate

1. Preheat the oven to 350°F. Line a cookie sheet with parchment paper. In a large, microwave-safe bowl, melt the butter, sugar, and brown sugar together in a microwave for 15 to 30 seconds on low power. Let the butter-sugar mixture cool just a bit then blend in the egg and egg yolk. Add the heavy cream and rose spread. Stir until just combined and set aside. Do not overmix.

2. In a medium bowl, sift together the flour, baking soda, and salt and carefully fold into the wet mixture. Gently add the chocolate, mixing well. Freeze the dough just until cold and firm, about 5 minutes.

3. Using a 2-ounce ice cream scoop, drop the dough 3 inches apart onto the prepared cookie sheet. Bake for 10 to 12 minutes, or until the edges of the cookies begin to brown. Transfer the cookies to a rack to cool.

Chai ka Crème Brûlée

CHAI-INFUSED CRÈME BRÛLÉE

- 1 1/2 cups water
- 6 green cardamom pods
- One 2-inch-long cinnamon stick
- 1/2 teaspoon black peppercorns
- 6 whole cloves
- 1 cup Darjeeling tea leaves
- 12 extra-large egg yolks
- 2 cups light brown sugar
- 4 cups heavy cream

For best results, I prepare the crème brûlée custards one day in advance to enhance the flavors of the spices and tea and then refrigerate them overnight. | serves 6

1. Place the water in a saucepan and add the cardamom, cinnamon, peppercorns, and cloves; bring to a boil. Add the tea leaves, reduce heat to low and simmer, 5 to 7 minutes. Strain out the tea leaves and spices using a fine strainer and then boil down the tea over high heat until it has reduced to 3/4 cup, about 10 minutes. Set aside to cool.

2. Preheat the oven to 325°F and place a kettle of water on high heat to boil. In a large, heatproof mixing bowl, whisk together the egg yolks and 1 cup of the sugar. Place the cream in a heavy-bottom saucepan over medium heat and heat until bubbles form around the edges. Remove from heat and, whisking constantly, pour into the egg and sugar mixture. Add the reduced tea mixture and continue whisking until the sugar has dissolved and the mixture is well combined, 5 to 7 minutes.

3. Strain the mixture through a very fine sieve and then pour evenly into 6 crème brûlée dishes or ramekins. Place the dishes in a roasting pan. Pour boiling water around the dishes or ramekins to reach halfway up the sides, then place the pan into the oven. Bake until custards are set around the edges but still jiggly in the centers, about 30 minutes. Remove the pan from the oven and let cool to room temperature. Remove the crème brûlée dishes from the pan and refrigerate until thoroughly chilled, at least 6 hours or overnight.

4. When ready to serve, preheat the broiler to high. Pass the remaining 1 cup brown sugar through a fine sieve to eliminate all lumps. Generously sprinkle the top of each dish with an equal portion of the brown sugar, taking care to cover all of the custard for an even finish. Place the dishes under the broiler and broil until the tops are caramelized or crackling brown, 4 to 6 minutes. Or, if using a torch to caramelize the custards, hold the torch at a 90° angle 3 to 4 inches from the surface of each dish, and use a steady sweeping motion to caramelize the tops until nicely browned. Serve immediately.

Chocolate aur Basmati chawal ka soufflé

CHOCOLATE BASMATI RICE SOUFFLÉ

Andrew Blackmore, friend and fellow chef, came up with this recipe by accident when he used my rice flour instead of all-purpose flour. Luckily he was in a hurry and didn't notice the mistake. Andrew's version of the classic soufflé is enhanced by the earthy flavor of the rice flour. Basmati rice flour isn't always easy to find: to make it yourself, grind the rice in a coffee or spice grinder then pass it through a fine sifter. | serves 6

6 ounces semisweet chocolate, chopped into even chunks

6 tablespoons unsalted butter

1/2 cup sugar

5 tablespoons basmati rice flour

1 cup whole milk

Pinch of salt

5 egg yolks, lightly beaten

1 teaspoon vanilla extract

7 egg whites

1. Place the chocolate in a dry, microwave-safe container. Melt the chocolate in the microwave: heat for 1 minute at half (50%) power. Remove from microwave and stir with a spatula. If the chocolate is not completely melted, put the chocolate in for another 30 seconds at half power. Stir and set aside to cool.

2. Preheat the oven to 400°F. Coat the bottom and sides of six 6-ounce ramekins with 2 tablespoons of the butter. Sprinkle the bottoms and sides evenly with the sugar. Tap out excess sugar and reserve for later use.

3. In a medium saucepan, melt the remaining 4 tablespoons butter. Stir in the basmati rice flour and cook, stirring occasionally, until the mixture begins to bubble, 3 to 4 minutes. Add the milk, melted chocolate, and salt. Cook over medium-low heat until the mixture thickens, stirring occasionally, about 5 minutes. Remove from heat and allow mixture to cool for 10 minutes. Whisk in beaten egg yolks and vanilla.

4. In a large bowl, beat the egg whites with an electric mixer until foamy. Gradually add the reserved sugar, beating until stiff. Fold the egg whites into the chocolate mixture. Gently spoon the mixture into prepared soufflé dishes. I like to sprinkle a little extra sugar on top of the soufflés to make them a little crustier.

5. Place the ramekins on a baking sheet and bake for 12 to 16 minutes or until puffed and browned. Serve immediately.

Collaborations

Over the years, I've had the chance to work with a lot of great people. Perhaps my most fruitful collaboration has been with the wonderful team at the Rubin Museum of Art. I met Shelley and Donald Rubin at a charity event and was immediately attracted to the vision of their museum. It is one of New York City's greatest cultural institutions and its dedication to the Himalayas makes it deeply precious to me. When Shelley invited me to cater an event at her home, I was glad to do it as it supported their work. This grew into other events as time went by. My work with their team, led by Special Events Manager Chris Phelan, has been inspiring.

The annual Nine Rivers Gala held at the museum honors individuals who have made major contributions to the Himalayan world. Gala dinners honoring the likes of former president Bill Clinton, Martha Stewart, the Queen of Bhutan, Sir Salman Rushdie, and Nobel Laureate Mohammed Yunus require menus that reflect the diversity of the Himalayas as well as the diversity of the museum's many supporters. Through the museum, I've also had the chance to work with extraordinary talents such as Jean-Georges Vongerichten of Jean Georges Restaurant and Eric Ripert of Le Bernardin. Never in my wildest dreams did I think I would be working with such towering talents, chefs who are among the greatest in the world. They have been even more generous with their time and talent than I could have wished.

I also work with the Rubin team on my favorite project, the Café at the Rubin Museum of Art, with the generous support of Shelley and Donald Rubin. The Café menu reflects my journeys in the Himalayas and my desire to share these spiritual adventures with the rest of the world. Oddly, the more I travel, the more centered and creative I feel. I grow and yet I am the same. The food is new yet the traditions remain—the center of the wheel remains fixed while we revolve around it, like a perfect mandala.

Gulab Jamun

GULAB JAMUN WITH COCONUT FLAKES

- 1 cup full-fat dry milk powder
- 2 tablespoons all-purpose flour
- 1 tablespoon semolina flour
- Pinch of baking powder
- 2 tablespoons ghee
- 6 1/2 tablespoons heavy cream
- Vegetable oil, for frying
- 1 cup sugar
- 1 cup water
- 6 drops rose water
- 1/2 cup sweetened coconut flakes

This famous Indian dessert, essentially a deep-fried milkball, similar to a donut, is often soaked in a thick sugar syrup. In this variation I roll it with coconut flakes and rose water. | serves 6

1. Sift together the milk powder, flour, semolina, and baking powder in a medium mixing bowl. Pour in the ghee and cream and hand-knead to a soft dough. Cover and set aside for 20 to 30 minutes.

2. Heat the oil, 3 inches deep, to 300°F in a heavy-bottomed frying pan. If you don't have a thermometer, drop a small piece of dough in the oil. If the dough bubbles immediately, the oil is ready. Line a sheet pan with paper towels. Divide the dough into 18 equal portions and roll into balls. Fry 6 to 8 balls at a time, turning frequently, until cooked through, 4 to 5 minutes. Remove with a slotted spoon and drain on lined sheetpan.

3. To make the syrup, bring the sugar, water, and rose water to a boil over high heat in a pot large enough to hold the fried balls. Remove from heat and add the fried balls to the syrup. Cover and let it sit until the fried balls are completely soaked in the syrup, about 15 minutes. Place the coconut flakes in a large bowl. Remove the fried balls from the syrup with a slotted spoon and toss them in the coconut flakes. Store in the refrigerator for up to 1 week. Serve at room temperature.

Adraki Nimboo ka Meetha

MEYER LEMON & GINGER COMPOTE

- 2 cups sugar
- 2 cups water
- One 1-inch-long piece cinnamon stick
- 6 black peppercorns
- 1 star anise
- 1/2 teaspoon ground cardamom
- 4 Meyer lemons
- 1 cup peeled, julienned fresh ginger

Meyer lemons are sweeter than other lemons and have a thinner peel with a floral scent. This light, refreshing compote can be served with ice cream or plain cake or as a stand-alone dessert. | serves 4

1. Prepare a simple syrup by combining the sugar, water, cinnamon, peppercorns, star anise, and cardamom in a heavy-bottom saucepan. Bring to a boil, reduce heat to low, and let simmer for 10 minutes.

2. Cut the lemons into 1/2-inch thick slices and poach them in the simmering syrup just until the rind is translucent, about 10 minutes. Remove the lemon slices with a slotted spoon and let them cool on a serving platter. Gently poach the ginger in the same syrup for 10 minutes and remove with a slotted spoon. Arrange the ginger over the lemon slices.

3. Increase the heat to high and boil the syrup until reduced by half, about 10 minutes. Let it cool to room temperature and then strain the syrup and ladle it gently over the poached lemon and ginger. Serve at room temperature for best flavor.

Rusbhari Kheer

RICE CUSTARD WITH GOLDEN BERRIES & HONEY

Golden berries, also known as cape gooseberries, are harvested in August and September. They have a papery outer skin that hides small, bittersweet, juicy berries. The parchment-like husk needs to be peeled back and rinsed before the berries can be used. I find that because of their piquant aftertaste golden berries also go nicely with meats and other savory foods. You may be able to find golden berries in season at your local farmers market. Gourmet shops may also carry them. | serves 6

- **1 cup basmati rice, rinsed under cold water, soaked for 1 hour, and drained**
- **9 cups whole milk**
- **1 teaspoon saffron threads**
- **1 vanilla bean, split and scraped**
- **3/4 cup plus 1 tablespoon sugar**
- **1 teaspoon ground cardamom**
- **1 1/2 cups halved golden berries, papery husks removed**
- **8 tablespoons (1 stick) butter**
- **2 tablespoons honey**

1. Place the rice in a blender along with 2 cups milk, and blend for about 1 minute. The mixture will still appear grainy.

2. Place the remaining 7 cups milk, along with the saffron and the vanilla bean and seeds in a large, heavy wok or saucepan and bring to a boil over medium heat. Reduce the heat to low and simmer, stirring and scraping constantly, until the milk has slightly thickened, 5 to 7 minutes.

3. Add the blended rice to the simmering milk, stirring with a whisk constantly to prevent any lumps. Increase the heat to medium-high and cook until the custard is thick and creamy, about 5 minutes. Add 3/4 cup sugar and the cardamom, reduce the heat to low, and cook for 5 minutes. Remove the vanilla bean and let the custard cool to room temperature, stirring often to prevent a skin from forming. Cover the custard and chill in the refrigerator for 4 hours or overnight before serving.

4. In a large, heavy-bottom saucepan over medium heat, combine the berries, butter, 1 tablespoon sugar, and the honey and cook until the berries are soft and the mixture is well combined and thick, about 5 minutes.

5. Serve the rice custard chilled with warm berries on the side.

Aam Santra aur Anar ka Mousse

MANGO & ORANGE MOUSSE WITH POMEGRANATE

1 1/4 cups canned mango purée (found at Indian groceries)
1 1/4 cups orange juice
3/4 cup sugar
1 tablespoon gelatin softened in 2 tablespoons water
3 cups heavy cream, whipped to stiff peaks
1/2 cup fresh pomegranate seeds, for garnish

If you can't find canned mango purée, you can make your own, but this dish tastes best with the distinctively Indian-flavored mangoes. Papayas are a good substitute for mangoes in this recipe. I usually make this dessert a day in advance and keep it refrigerated. | serves 6

1. In a saucepan, heat the mango purée, orange juice, and sugar over medium-low heat, stirring constantly until the sugar has dissolved. Add the gelatin and stir to melt and combine.

2. Strain the mango mixture into a bowl and place it over an ice bath. Stir occasionally with a rubber spatula and when it just starts to set, after about 20 minutes, fold in the whipped cream. Cover with plastic wrap and refrigerate for at least 4 hours or overnight.

3. Serve chilled, garnished with pomegranate seeds.

Ananas aur Saunf Crème Anglaise

PAN-SEARED PINEAPPLE WITH FENNEL CRÈME ANGLAISE

In this recipe, sweet pineapple is crusted with sugar and coarsely ground peppercorns, then seared until golden. The spicy bursts of pepper are perfectly tempered by the sweet fruit and rich crème anglaise. | serves 6 to 8

FOR THE CRÈME ANGLAISE

- 4 egg yolks
- 1/2 cup sugar
- 1 cup heavy cream
- 1 cup whole milk
- 1 1/2 tablespoons sour cream
- 1 whole vanilla bean, split lengthwise
- 1 teaspoon ground fennel

FOR THE PINEAPPLE

- 1 ripe pineapple, peeled, cored, and sliced into 3/4-inch-thick rounds
- 3 tablespoons sugar
- 2 teaspoons Tellicherry or other black peppercorns, coarsely ground
- 1 tablespoon vegetable oil

1. To make the crème anglaise, use a whisk to blend together the egg yolks and sugar in a medium mixing bowl until they are pale yellow and smooth.

2. In a heavy-bottom pan, combine the cream, milk, sour cream, vanilla bean, and fennel and bring to a simmer over medium heat. Whisk about half the hot cream mixture into the egg yolk mixture until well combined, then stir this back into the saucepan. Over medium heat, stirring constantly with a wooden spoon, cook the mixture until it is thick enough to coat the back of the spoon, about 5 minutes. Strain into a clean bowl and set the bowl over an ice bath until chilled, stirring occasionally. Refrigerate, covered, until needed.

3. To prepare the pineapple, generously sprinkle both sides of the pineapple with sugar and peppercorns. Set aside.

4. Preheat a heavy skillet (cast iron is best) over medium-high heat. When it is hot, add as little vegetable oil as possible to cover the bottom of the skillet. Sear the pineapple on both sides and remove to serving plates.

5. Serve the pineapple warm with the chilled crème anglaise on the side.

Pista Phirni

INDIAN RICE PUDDING WITH PISTACHIOS & SILVER LEAVES

- 1 cup basmati rice, rinsed, soaked for 1 hour, and drained
- 8 cups whole milk
- 1 teaspoon saffron threads
- 1/2 cup skinned, raw almonds, coarsely chopped
- 1 teaspoon ground cinnamon
- 3/4 cup sugar
- 1 teaspoon ground cardamom
- 1 cup canned mango purée (found at Indian groceries)
- 6 silver leaves (found at Indian groceries)
- 3 tablespoons pistachio slivers, for garnish

Edible silver leaf, finer than tissue paper, is used in Indian cuisine to garnish special festive dishes on grand occasions. Also known as *varak*, it can be purchased at Indian specialty food shops and some art suppliers. It is made from pure silver, small blocks of which are interleaved with paper, wrapped in leather, and then beaten with a constant, drumming action (which effectively puts a stop to conversation if one is anywhere near the shops which make it) until uniformly thin. | serves 6

1. Place the rice in a blender along with 2 cups of the milk and blend for about 1 minute. The mixture will appear grainy.

2. Place the remaining 6 cups milk, the saffron, and almonds in a large, heavy wok or saucepan and bring to a boil over high heat. Reduce the heat to medium and simmer, stirring and scraping constantly, until the milk has slightly thickened, 5 to 7 minutes.

3. Add the blended rice to the simmering milk, whisking constantly to prevent lumps. Increase the heat to medium-high and cook, stirring, until the custard is thick and creamy, about 5 minutes. Stir in the cinnamon, sugar, cardamom, and mango purée and reduce the heat to low, cooking until the pudding is thick and the flavors have blended, 8 to 10 minutes. Gently pour into 6 small serving dishes and top each one with a silver leaf.

4. Serve warm or at room temperature, garnished with pistachios.

DRINKS

Every meal made in my kitchen is accompanied by the right beverage, whether it comes at the start of, during, or end of the meal. I grew up in typical Indian fashion where meals were often followed by chai, which in India is the generic term for tea.

...

In this section, I have included drinks that range from savory to sweet. These drink recipes can be made to cool the spirit on a hot evening or warm your guests up on chilly nights. Pair them with your favorite recipes from this book to add an extra bit of balance to your meals.

ROSE AND CARDAMOM SUMMER DRINK

CUMIN WATER WITH MINT AND TAMARIND

MASALA LASSI WITH TOASTED CUMIN

INDIAN LIMEADE WITH CHAAT MASALA

SPICY HIMALAYAN CHAI

CHAMOMILE TEA

MOROCCAN MINT GUNPOWDER TEA

MANGO LASSI

HONEY-STRAWBERRY TEA COOLER

FROZEN GUAVA SPRITZER WITH LIME JUICE

SAFFRON AND ALMOND MILK

ROSE-SCENTED GREEN TEA

Gulabi Thanda

ROSE & CARDAMOM SUMMER DRINK

- 7 1/2 cups water
- 6 green cardamom pods
- 6 drops rose essence (extract)
- 1 cup sugar
- Juice of 1 lemon
- 1/2 teaspoon red food coloring, if desired

This drink, based on the Turkish sherbet, is traditionally served on hot summer nights. The word sherbet was originally a Turkish word that referred to a sweetened fruit drink, often mixed with snow from the mountains. Rose essence, which is a more concentrated form of rose water, should be added sparingly because it has a very strong floral aroma and taste. | serves 6

1. In a medium pot over high heat, combine the water, cardamom, and rose essence; bring to a boil. Reduce heat to low and simmer until the flavors are well combined, 5 minutes.

2. Stir in the sugar until dissolved. Remove from heat, add lemon juice and red food coloring, if using, and let cool to room temperature, about 1 hour.

3. Pour over ice and serve chilled.

Jal Jeera

CUMIN WATER WITH MINT & TAMARIND

Black salt is an essential ingredient in this recipe, a beloved summer drink in India because of its cooling properties. The drink, called *jal jeera* in Hindi, is sold at many roadside stands during hot weather. | serves 6

- 2 tablespoons cumin seeds, dry-roasted (see page 17) and ground fine
- 2 tablespoons finely chopped fresh mint leaves, plus 12 leaves for garnish
- 2 tablespoons finely chopped fresh cilantro leaves
- 1 tablespoon mango powder
- 1/2 teaspoon black salt or sea salt
- 2 tablespoons tamarind paste
- 1/2 teaspoon sugar
- 5 cups water

In a large mixing bowl combine all the ingredients. Refrigerate for at least 2 hours before serving. To serve, stir well, pour over ice, and garnish with mint leaves.

Jeera wali Lassi

MASALA LASSI WITH TOASTED CUMIN

3 cups plain, lowfat yogurt
1 cup water
1/2 teaspoon salt
1 tablespoon cumin seeds, dry-roasted (see page 17) and ground
Mint sprigs, for garnish

Lassi is a popular Indian drink traditionally made by blending yogurt, sugar, and spices. I have added cumin to flavor the *lassi* in this recipe and omitted the sugar for a savory drink. Toasting the cumin seeds releases their essential oils and imparts a warm aroma. | **serves 4 to 6**

Combine the yogurt, water, and salt in a blender until frothy. Pour over ice and serve chilled, sprinkled with ground cumin and mint sprigs.

Masala Nimboo Paani

INDIAN LIMEADE WITH CHAAT MASALA

- 2 cups sugar
- 1 cup hot water
- 2 cups fresh lime juice
- 1 cup cold water
- 2 tablespoons *chaat masala* (page 20)
- 1 lime, thinly sliced, for garnish

Lime juice and water sweetened with sugar and seasoned with *chaat masala* makes a refreshing drink on a hot summer day. The flavors are a good balance between sweet and tart. The limeade can also be blended with ice to make a frozen drink. | serves 4

Place the sugar and hot water in a large container and stir until the sugar dissolves. Add the lime juice, cold water, and *chaat masala.* Stir until well mixed. Chill in the refrigerator until ready to serve. Pour over glasses of ice, squeeze a slice of lime on top of each glass, and serve chilled.

Meeting Gordon

When I received a call from a complete stranger telling me that Chef Gordon Ramsay wanted my help, I knew that the course of my life was about to change. I knew that *Hell's Kitchen* was one of the most famous television shows about cooking there had ever been. Now Gordon needed my help with a struggling Indian restaurant in Manhattan for a new show. I admit I was reluctant. I just wasn't sure that my style of leadership would mesh well with Gordon's. The producers of the show were persistent and I finally agreed to meet with them and Gordon.

When we met, I explained my concerns and found Gordon to be remarkably sensitive and compassionate. He was not at all what I expected based on his public persona. Gordon does set very high standards, but he sets them even higher for himself, never asking anything of anyone that he wouldn't do himself. He is thoughtful, generous in the extreme, and has one of the most intensely loyal teams in the business. When he explained that this was an opportunity to take on a failing business and set it right again, I was intrigued. *Kitchen Nightmares* was to be an intervention show in which he gave restaurants some tough love and encouraged them to do things better in order to save their businesses. My role was to bring the team together and teach them to work as one to make and serve great food. I agreed to do what I could to help.

When I went to the restaurant and saw that it was indeed in terrible crisis, I felt deep compassion for a team that needed new leadership to turn it around. After all the work was done and it was time to decide the future of the restaurant, Gordon asked if I were willing to commit to seeing it through and provide ongoing consulting services. Having promised him, I stayed and continued to give them new focus while continuing my own work with the Café at the Rubin Museum; my catering business, Flavors and Feasts; and my charity group, SAKIV. I now count Gordon as one of the best friends a cook could have. Whenever we meet, my inspiration is renewed and I consider myself fortunate to have made such a friend.

Tez Himalayan Chai

SPICY HIMALAYAN CHAI

- 1 tablespoon fennel seeds
- 6 green cardamom pods
- 12 whole cloves
- One 1-inch-long piece cinnamon stick
- One 1-inch-long piece fresh ginger, peeled and coarsely chopped
- 2 bay leaves
- 5 black peppercorns
- 6 cups water
- 3 tablespoons loose Darjeeling tea leaves
- 1 cup whole milk

Darjeeling teas are immensely popular and are regarded as the finest of black teas in India. It is generally a light afternoon tea, but that lightness depends on what time of year the leaves are harvested and the age of the dried leaves. The leaves that are harvested earlier always have a lighter bouquet. I have yet to find a similarly perfect flavor and aroma in any other variety of tea. | makes 6 cups

Place all the ingredients except the tea leaves and milk in a medium pot over high heat and bring it to boil. Add the tea leaves, reduce heat to low, and simmer for 5 minutes; add the milk. Bring to a boil and reduce the heat again to low. Simmer for 2 minutes, strain, and serve immediately.

Babun Phool Chai

CHAMOMILE TEA

- 6 cups water
- 6 teaspoons dried chamomile flowers
- 3 teaspoons honey
- Juice of 1 lemon

One of the oldest herbs, the chamomile flower is not just a pretty flower, it also makes a wonderful brew. Chamomile tea is a caffeine-free herbal tea and has a reputation for being a soothing and calming drink. The finest variety of chamomile comes from Egypt. | makes 6 cups

1. Bring the water to the boil in a saucepan with a lid. Sprinkle the flowers onto the water and boil, covered, for 30 seconds. Remove from the heat and let stand for 1 minute.

2. Stir in the honey and lemon juice and serve. You may pour the tea through a strainer to remove the flowers, but I prefer to leave the flowers in.

Pudinewali Chai

MOROCCAN MINT GUNPOWDER TEA

4 cups water
10 fresh mint sprigs, plus 4 for garnish
3 teaspoons gunpowder tea
3 tablespoons sugar

Gunpowder tea is a form of green tea produced in the Zhejiang province of China. It is made of green tea leaves hand-rolled into tiny pellets that resemble gunpowder, giving this tea its distinctive name. Gunpowder tea is used in the preparation of the popular Moroccan mint tea, an important part of the tea ritual in Morocco and other parts of North Africa. If you have Moroccan guests, serve additional sugar on the side. | serves 4

In a medium pot, boil the water. Pour a small amount into a teapot and swish around to warm the pot. Combine the mint, tea, and sugar in the teapot and then add the rest of the hot water. Let the tea brew, stirring the leaves once or twice, for 3 minutes. Pour tea through a tea strainer into glass teacups. Garnish with remaining sprigs of mint and serve.

Aam wali Lassi

MANGO LASSI

- 3 cups plain, lowfat yogurt
- 1 cup canned mango purée, (found at Indian groceries)
- 1/2 cup whole milk
- 1/2 cup water
- 1/4 cup sugar

This popular Indian drink hardly needs an introduction. Its smooth, creamy texture goes perfectly with Indian food and it is quick and easy to make. Indian mangoes have a very special flavor all their own, and it's worth going out of your way to find Indian mango purée. You can also substitute mango with your favorite fruits such as bananas or peaches. My sister Radhika prefers this made with vanilla-flavored yogurt. | serves 4 to 6

Combine all the ingredients in a blender until smooth and frothy. Pour over ice and serve chilled.

Shahd Thandi Chai

HONEY-STRAWBERRY TEA COOLER

- 6 cups water
- 6 tea bags green tea
- 6 tablespoons honey
- 1/2 cup fresh lemon juice, plus 2 whole lemons cut into thin rings
- 1 pint strawberries, stemmed, cleaned, and sliced
- 1/3 cup fresh mint leaves

This drink can be made with different flavors of green tea. To brew green tea, I always bring the water to a simmer, not a boil. If the water does come to a boil, it should be allowed to settle for forty-five to sixty seconds before preparing to prevent the tea from becoming bitter. | serves 6

1. In a medium saucepan, bring the water to a simmer, add the tea bags, and let steep for 2 to 2 1/2 minutes. Remove the tea bags and add the honey and lemon juice. Remove from heat and let cool to room temperature. Add the strawberries and mint. Refrigerate for at least 2 hours.

2. Serve over crushed ice.

Amrood ka Thanda

FROZEN GUAVA SPRITZER WITH LIME JUICE

- 4 ripe guavas
- Juice of 3 limes
- 3 tablespoons honey
- 2 cups ice
- 3 cups seltzer

An alternative to lemonade, this summer cooler brings the flavor of the tropics to your lips. Cold and refreshing, this beverage has a nice pale green color, and the consistency after blending the guava with ice is almost like slush. Fresh mint leaves may be added for a twist. | serves 6

Cut the guavas in half lengthwise, scoop out the pulp and purée it in a blender with the lime juice, honey, ice, and seltzer until smooth. Serve chilled.

Thandai

SAFFRON & ALMOND MILK

7 1/2 cups whole milk
1/2 cup flaked almonds
1 teaspoon saffron threads, plus 2 pinches for garnish
1 teaspoon ground cardamom
6 tablespoons honey

Saffron threads give this flavorful and soothing milk its beautiful orange-yellow color. Saffron in milk has been popular for centuries. For me, this drink is a quintessential part of celebrations in India. This milk is served hot or warm, particularly during festivals. | serves 6

Bring the milk to a boil in a medium pot over high heat. Reduce the heat to low and add the almonds, saffron, cardamom, and honey. Simmer, stirring, until all the ingredients are well combined, about 5 minutes. Serve hot, garnished with saffron.

5 cups water
1/2 cup dried rose petals and buds
Juice of 1 lemon
1/4 cup loose green tea
3 tablespoons sugar

Gulabi Hari Chai

ROSE-SCENTED GREEN TEA

Roses are deliciously edible flowers with an exotic flavor. The darker petals usually have more flavor, while the white portion of the petal is generally bitter. Dried petals give a delicate fragrance to this tea. Even non–tea drinkers will love it. | serves 4

1. Bring 3 cups of water to a boil in a medium pot. Add the rose petals and lemon juice, then turn off the heat and allow the mixture to sit for 5 to 6 minutes. Strain and return the rose water to the pot.

2. Meanwhile, bring the remaining 2 cups water to a boil, remove from heat, and add the tea leaves. Let it steep for 5 minutes and then strain into the rose-flavored water.

3. Stir in the sugar until dissolved and simmer for another 2 minutes. Serve hot or chilled over ice.

Epilogue: Now and for the Future

For the past couple of years, while working on other projects, I have assembled my own team of trusted people who share my vision of doing more for the world than just cooking in restaurants. We have been writing books, including this one, which relate all that I have learned about food and sharing. We have worked at documenting Himalayan cuisine, specifically the foodways of the common people, to preserve it for future generations in the upcoming book *Return to the Rivers*. We also conceived the idea of a series of films, *Holy Kitchens*, which tell the story of how people of different faiths share food in the name of God. This film series is meant to show people how much we all have in common and to encourage mutual understanding and tolerance as well as to explore the role of food in creating a sense of community. Our first film on Sikhism premiered in New York City in the fall of 2010, and we are well on our way to sharing a new vision of the unique and special place of food in religion.

We are bringing all of this experience to bear in our next restaurant project: Junoon. This restaurant celebrates the glories of Indian cuisine and hospitality. It is our hope that this will be a great place to work as well as a great place to eat. We source our ingredients locally, using primarily organic ingredients, work with the seasons, and make everything fresh, every day. It has been one of the greatest pleasures of my career to work with Rajesh Bhardwaj, who shares my passion for excellence. We look forward to helping Indian cuisine establish a reputation for quality that rivals those of the world's great cuisines. So many wonderful things have happened to me in my life that I can't even begin to imagine what else will come up. If you had asked me when I was ten years old what I thought would happen to me in the future, I would have told you that I would just want to make a nice pot of lentils for my family to eat. I still want that.

SOURCES

There are number of great shops where you can buy fresh herbs and spices. I've listed a few of my favorites here, many of which allow you to shop online as well. I also suggest looking around for an Indian grocery in your neighborhood.

Kalustyan's
123 Lexington Ave.
New York, NY 10016
212-685-3451
800-352-3451
www.kalustyans.com

Patel Brothers
multiple locations
www.patelbrothers.com

Apna Bazar Cash & Carry
7200 37th Ave.
Flushing, NY 11372
718-565-5960

My Spice Sage
877-890-5244
www.myspicesage.com

Spice Corner
135 Lexington Ave.
New York, NY 10016
212-689-5182
www.spicecorner29.com

House of Spices
718-507-4900
www.hosindia.com

The Spice House
1512 N. Wells St.
Chicago, IL 60610
312-274-0378
www.thespicehouse.com

PHOTO CREDITS

RECIPE CREDITS

INDEX

C

D

R

S